healing

connections

About the author:
    Kathleen J. is a university professor in Texas. This is her first book about recovery.

healing
connections

*sharing
the recovery
journey*

kathleen j.

■ᴿᴹ HAZELDEN®

First published February 1990.

Library of Congress Card Catalog Number: 89-85746

ISBN: 0-89486-615-X

Printed in the United States of America.

Editor's note:
   Hazelden Education Materials offers a variety of informa-
tion on chemical dependency and related areas. Our publica-
tions do not necessarily represent Hazelden or its programs,
nor do they officially speak for any Twelve Step organization.

Contents

Preface

Every recovering alcoholic tells a story of transformation. Like the song "Amazing Grace," we sing, "I once was lost but now I'm found, was blind but now I see."

On one level, what I'm about to tell is another story of being lost and then found, of having been blind and now seeing. On another level, it is a story of a journey, a journey of healing connections.

On this journey I have been guided and comforted by the wisdom and strength of other recovering people. Through them I have learned how to make connections within myself, with other people, and with a Higher Power.

When I was first trying to quit drinking, I needed all the reassurance I could get. I read the stories in the Big Book over and over, trying to find out as much as I could about what it was like for these men and women who had quit drinking and who had found a new way of life. I was scared and shaky and needed to be reassured that there was a way out, that recovery was possible and worth it.

What I liked most about the stories was that they each described a transformation — a miracle that had been worked as each person learned how to stay sober, One Day at a Time. I desperately needed the exuberance and energy that these stories of transformation offered. I relied on their implicit promise that there was another way to feel and be.

But the transformations in these stories seemed sudden and mysterious. For years, these people had struggled with drinking, were trapped in misery, and now, suddenly, they were whole, healthy, and free. They seemed to have slipped, overnight, from agony to ecstasy. I couldn't understand how the miracle had been pulled off.

It felt then like they were on the other side of a divide, waving to me and saying, "It's great over here!" It seemed to me that the path across, and how it felt on the road they'd traveled to get there, was never fully explained or described. All I could hear was that the road to recovery had something to do with not taking the first drink, surrendering, cleaning house, seeking God, and living One Day at a Time.

I wanted to know how this miracle of recovery from alcoholism was pulled off. I wanted to know how it felt, getting from drunkeness to sobriety. What was it like, living sober year after year? As I continued in recovery, discovering all kinds of unexpected, scary and confusing feelings, new and frightening desires, I wanted to learn more about the journey itself.

In recovery, I have often felt fear, confusion, and doubt. Sometimes I have been discouraged; all my efforts to work the program, to become well, have seemed useless and futile. Then, especially, the stories of other recovering men and women remind me that I am not alone.

What continues to help me most in recovery, and what I hope I can offer you in this book, is the wisdom of those who have shared this journey with me. They have had the same doubts and fears and felt the same joys and pains. Because they have shared their experiences with me, they have freed me to experience my own recovery, to make my own connections within myself, to them, and to a Higher Power.

The recovering people in my life don't talk of a sudden redemption, or describe their recovery as an automatic transformation. They tell me, honestly and truthfully, about a *journey* of renewal. They describe for me passages through new and sometimes frightening terrain. They, along with me, are learning how to be sober, how to live without alcohol, but they are also learning how to live, how to grow and change.

I knew that to quit drinking, I had to work the Twelve Steps. But it has been through the love, support, and guidance of other recovering people that I have learned ways to live more happily than I could ever have imagined. For me, recovery

2

from alcoholism has been so much more than not drinking. The recovery journey has meant healing old wounds, making new connections, cultivating spiritual faith, and becoming whole, and as I've already said, making new connections. I gained the wisdom and courage that makes all of this possible through other people in the program.

When I was first getting sober, it was hard for me to reach out to strangers, even if they reminded me of me. But I was always willing to read — especially when my life became painful, confusing, and difficult. I don't know who you are reading this book, but I hope my words can help you in your recovery journey.

If you are wondering if you really are an alcoholic, I hope my story shows you that being a recovering alcoholic can be a blessing. If you know that drinking is causing you trouble, but you don't know if you can or want to quit, I hope my experiences show you what's possible with abstinence.

If you are in the beginning of your own recovery, full of the excitement and doubt that comes at the beginning of any trip into the unknown, I hope my story helps you find your own best path.

I am grateful for the words of the honest and loving men and women who have helped me grow. I pray that they speak to you, through me, and that we can help you find yourself in recovery.

PART I

FINDING RECOVERY

Addiction blinds us to the true causes of our pain. In the beginning, it tells us that there are easy ways out, that we can find solace in temporary escapes. Later, it tells us that our problems are caused by other people, places, and things, that our addiction is a natural response to an unnatural world. Finally, addiction tells us that we can't live without it, that to give up our addiction is to give up our lives. Recovery from addiction requires breaking through denial. This is how it was for me, finding recovery.

CHAPTER ONE

The Starting Place

I call my recovery a journey because it feels as if I lived for years in a narrow, confining, chaotic place, and then gradually, hesitantly learned how to leave that place, and walk into a wider world of feelings, people, and new experiences. I began that journey trapped in a way of life that was becoming less happy, more empty, and ever more painful and frightening.

Healing the Day's Wounds with Alcohol

It may sound like my life was unmitigated hell, but it wasn't. There were moments of joy, friendship, and hope. There came a point, though, when those moments were harder and harder to come by. My life, by the time I stopped drinking, had become a tremendous effort.

Everything seemed to loom dark and foreboding. I remember getting up in the morning, aching, hungover, trying to shower away the poisons that seemed to clog my pores. I would stare at myself in the mirror, searching for the courage to walk out the door and face the dangerous and unexpected. I would come home to collapse, exhausted by the effort of surviving the day.

I was exhausted by the effort of being my "best self," a self that was increasingly false. My real self seemed at times to be a lost, hurt, frightened child, and at other times a harsh, bitter woman who surfaced at 3:00 a.m. to taunt me.

Was I ever at peace? Yes, but toward the end it was only after the third drink, just before the fourth. For that brief moment, I was at peace, but I could never stop there. I would keep on drinking, and my sense of peace, of connectedness, would disappear in a fog of blurred feelings that could, at any moment, erupt and take me over. The next day, I would wake to the knowledge that once again I had gotten drunk and lost my bearings. I would shower, pull myself together, and go off and do my best to survive the day.

That was what life was like during the last few years of my drinking. Each of us has a different pattern. Mine was to drink daily so I could unwind and heal the day's wounds. That I almost always got drunk, that I felt wretched the next day, and that my life was a constant attempt to recover from the night before did not really register with me.

I knew that I drank differently than my friends, but I always had. My problem, I came to believe, was that I hadn't yet figured out how to bounce back, how to get the proper balance of exercise, nutrition, sleep, and alcohol to wake up and feel good the next day. What I needed in my life, I believed, was balance, but somehow I could never achieve it.

Playing the Sensitive Artist

There seemed an even deeper difference between me and my friends, those "other people" whose lives seemed smooth and untroubled, cheerful and content. I believed that I was a sensitive, poetic artist, while they were dull and simple-minded. I explained my increasingly desperate life as the only possible one for someone so sensitive. I found plenty of confirmation for this belief in the biographies of people, brilliant and creative, who destroyed themselves with drink. Even though I was living their life, I tried to ignore the fact that I was not writing anything creative or brilliant. I kept drinking, and wrote endlessly about myself, my discontent, my loneliness, my exhaustion.

I have boxes full of the poems, stories, and journals I wrote in those last years. They were my talisman and my release, the way I justified myself to myself. They are painful to reread. They are all the same, although I did not see that at the time. They are a record of my search for myself, and they are an agonizing account of helplessness. Seemingly new insights, new ways to be, and new modes of understanding are juxtaposed with lost days and nights, drunken rages and pain. Time after time, year after year, I would have the same revelation: I was suffering needlessly; I had found a way out; I would try a new path, and all would be well.

Not drinking was rarely the way out I tried. It was sometimes a sidelight, along with a healthy regimen of regular meals, exercise, fresh air, and a disciplined schedule. It was the deep truths that I thought would liberate me. What were these truths? Nothing very earthshaking — simple things like being true to myself, honest about my feelings, accepting of others, in tune with the secret harmony of life.

What pains me when I reread those pages is how much I knew in my head about living a better life, but how impossible it was for me to accomplish. Simple acts of courage and faith, basic qualities like honesty, acceptance, and trust continued to elude me. And so I kept struggling. Those handwritten pages are a testament to how trapped I was.

Nothing to Say to the Happy and Productive

Active alcoholism prevents us from changing ourselves. No matter how desperately we seek to escape and to grow, practicing our addiction blocks us from it. Our best efforts only lead us down blind alleys. Our most fervent prayers for solace are answered only by more anxiety and despair.

On the few occasions I have the strength and desire to find her again, I have mixed feelings about the woman I meet when I reread those pages of my writing. Part of me aches for her, so full of pain, so lost and confused. Part of me is angry at her for being so blind, for knowing that she was drinking every day, getting drunk when she didn't want to, and still she kept on. And part of me is proud of her, for the brave, pathetic way she kept on searching. But what frightens me is that sometimes I still miss her; my addiction is not just to alcohol, but also to a kind of existential unhappiness that was her natural element.

One of the biggest barriers to my recovery has been that I once believed that despair was a more authentic human condition than happiness. The people I admired most seemed deep and mysterious. The writers I read were torn by conflict; the philosophers I studied were forever engaged with darker forces; the friends I sought were the walking wounded, baffled and battered by life.

I had nothing to say to the happy and productive; they seemed to live in another world. And they had nothing to say to me, or at least nothing I would listen to. When they forced their way into my life, they would tell me that I took myself too seriously, that I seemed to delight in being miserable, and that I always saw the darker side. *Yes,* I would mutter to myself, *I see things that you can't even grasp — the true essence of life.* And I would go back to my books about tortured poets and women on the edge of madness, listen to my songs about loss and despair, and believe myself to be among kindred spirits.

I tell you this because I need to explain, to you and to myself, why I was so unwilling to accept help. I held on to my pain with a grip that seems desperate in its intensity. Why would anyone want to keep living in a way that guarantees pain when around her are other ways to live, ways that obviously work so much better? There are probably as many reasons for this as there are people suffering from addiction. For me, the justification was that hurting *was* really living. Being happy was being shallow, using a bunch of clichés to float through life.

With this attitude, you can understand how I could suspect that I was alcoholic and still keep on drinking. This belief allowed me to know about AA and reject it; it also allowed me to fight my own recovery, even after I quit drinking. Let me tell you a little of my story, and you'll see how my denial worked.

CHAPTER TWO

My Story

I started drinking in high school. It was the late 1960s, and most of my friends were experimenting with drugs. I preferred to drink because liquor felt more friendly to me, not "really" a drug. I felt more in control with alcohol; I had a tremendous capacity, and felt at home, at ease, when I drank. I developed a pattern of daily drinking that did not seem to be affecting my life at all. It became, simply, the way I lived.

Before my senior year in college, a friend of mine suddenly went off to an alcoholism treatment center. He came back declaring that he was an alcoholic, and that he could never drink again. I was appalled. He was a playwright, a tortured poet-type like myself, and here he was, spouting hokey phrases like Let Go and Let God, One Day At a Time, Easy Does It, and the like. I figured he'd been brainwashed.

Playing the Recovering Person

Besides that, he began hinting that I drank like him and that I couldn't quit drinking on my own. To disprove this, I vowed to quit. It was the first time in six years that I tried to change my drinking pattern. I couldn't. By the third day I was jumping out of my skin, irritable and frightened. I decided that I was, perhaps, alcohol-dependent, and went with him to an outpatient clinic to talk to a counselor.

She gave me a battery of tests. Among them was the "Ten Questions" test that appears every so often in the newspaper. I had taken it already, answering yes to five or six of the questions, only to discover at the bottom that if I answered yes to more than three, I was definitely an alcoholic. I was outraged by what I thought was a stupid, biased test. So, in the office, I decided to prove to them that, while I may have unintentionally become physically dependent on alcohol, I was by *no means* an alcoholic.

In taking her tests, I shaded the truth as much as I could. Nonetheless, my scores indicated that I was a genuine alcoholic. I dismissed this label — after all, the place needed clients to stay in business, right? The counselor recommended regular AA meetings, outpatient counseling, and group therapy. I complied. I was a people-pleaser, and I suspect I was also intrigued by the prospect of delving into my complicated psyche. I began what turned into nine months without alcohol.

I remember very little of my treatment. I know that I ridiculed the pop psychology language of therapy — the "warm fuzzies" and "getting in touch with your feelings." I thought that the few AA meetings I attended were crowded, smoky, boring, and full of people who were too cheerful to be real. But I went along with it and felt pretty darn proud of myself. I had kicked the habit and joined the unhooked generation. I finished the school year, and was accepted to graduate school in another state. I packed and got ready to move with the sense that I had learned a valuable lesson. I had "stopped in time," and was ready to go off into a new, adult life.

I got drunk the night before I left. When I arrived, I was scared and alone. I tried not to drink, but a little wine with dinner helped me relax. I called AA late one night and went to a nearby meeting, but there I saw only tired old men complaining about how hard it was not to drink. I decided that I had learned enough about alcoholism to control my drinking, to create a life that could include but not be run by alcohol. I would "keep an eye on it," and if it ever got out of control, I would quit again. I'd done it once, hadn't I?

Still an Alcoholic

They talk in AA about the imaginary line that we cross, a line that, once we cross it, means we can never go back to social drinking again. I had clearly crossed that line, but I was unable to recognize it. Instead, I spent the next seven years in an increasingly desperate attempt to control my drinking and my life.

During that time, I stayed in graduate school, even though every semester I vowed to drop out and find something more rewarding to do. But I dimly knew that without the structure of school I would go completely out of control. The routine of semesters, classes, assignments, and grades kept me functioning. It was the ballast that kept me on an even keel.

I began to lead a double life — the division between day and night was also a division of my self. During the day I was a good, if uneven, student. I got to my classes and I talked about ideas. I read my assignments and I wrote my papers in a desperate flash, trying to get it all done so I could have time for myself at night. Time for myself was time to drink, although I never defined it that way. How I used my time changed over the years as I tried to find ways to keep drinking and still meet my responsibilities.

Sometimes it was the night life that appealed to me, going out to dance and listen to jazz. Sometimes it was sitting at home alone in my robe, listening to Billie Holiday sing the blues. Sometimes it was having people over, talking late into the night. Finally, it became one bar, a place with live country music and a world I felt a part of.

I fell in love with that bar and spent most of my last few drinking years in it. It seemed like a magical place, soft and comforting. With all the cry-in-your-beer songs about heartache, sorrow, and love gone wrong, it felt like home. I was known there, and felt special. I was "family," part of a group of hardworking people who deserved a night on the town, drinking, dancing, and talking with friends. Eventually, I was hired as a barmaid. After closing time, I'd sit with the other employees and drink for hours, for free.

It was a captivating other life, one that puzzled my friends from school. So I kept my lives separate. By then, I had three lives — student, barmaid, and the writer, turning out endless pages of journals, trying to sort out who I was, where I fit in, and how I could escape.

Making a Rational Decision
to Crawl to the Bathroom

I haven't told the gory drunk stories all us alcoholics have
— throwing up on people's lawns . . . getting beaten up by
boyfriends . . . having the police report me missing to my
college dean . . . shaking in public restrooms, too frightened to
leave . . . trying to teach a class when I was too hungover to
read my notes . . . crawling to the bathroom in the middle of
the night. I'm not proud of these things, but they did happen,
even when I was trying to make sure my drinking didn't get
"out of control." I refused to accept that these events meant
anything. They were awful moments, but they could be erased
and glossed over simply by turning over the new leaf that was
always out there, ready to be turned.

I will, however, tell you more about my crawls to the bathroom, only because they show how strong my denial was, and
how carefully I constructed my life to prove that I was still in
control of my drinking. Every night, before I went out, I would
make sure that my apartment was in perfect order and that
there was nothing on the floor waiting to trip me upon my
return. In fact, the worse my drinking got, the more orderly I
became. To misplace my keys, have dishes in the sink, or
clothes on the floor, would have been a sure sign I was losing
my grip. I'd seen those movies about alcoholics. They were
always unshaven and lived in crummy tenements with empty
bottles everywhere and half-eaten cans of beans moldering in
the kitchen sink.

That wasn't me. No sir! I had my surroundings so in order
that when I got home, woozy and blurred, I could gracefully
get ready for bed, with the kitchen gleaming, the bedroom neat,
the world under my control. I could walk right to the bed
without stumbling over anything because I'd cleared the path
so I had a straight shot from the door.

I would throw my clothes in the hamper, put on a night-
gown, and lie down for sleep. Sometimes I passed out. Sometimes I would just lie there, the room spinning. Eventually, I
would somehow make it to the bathroom to throw up.

I really did not believe, until I was several months sober, that I had ever crawled anywhere in a drunken stupor. In meetings, people would describe their drinking days and talk about such behavior while I shook my head in disbelief. How could anyone sink so low? When *I* had to throw up in the middle of the night, I made a conscious and rational decision to crawl, a decision with my safety in mind. Since I was usually a little dizzy, the safest and most efficient way to get from the bed to the toilet was on my hands and knees. I told myself it wasn't crawling; it was simply the most appropriate mode of transport.

That was the way my denial worked. I reinterpreted all the signs that drinking was destroying my life. I was not crawling; I was safety conscious. I was not miserable; I was in tune with the despair of the universe. I was not working in a bar so I could get free drinks; I was sharing in a "real world experience." I was not getting drunk every night; I was simply drinking too much sometimes. And yes, I had been diagnosed an alcoholic, but on those stupid tests, any real drinker would come out that way.

A clear-eyed look at my life was impossible. I knew that I was running out of time, that school would come to an end and I needed, as I put it, to decide what I wanted to be when I grew up. And I had no idea who I was, or what I wanted.

Pardon the Cliché-Spouting Robot

Ironically, it was my intense desire to rescue others that finally brought me to seriously join AA's fellowship of recovering men and women. In my last summer of drinking, when I had cleared the decks for "real work" and ended up drinking all night and sleeping all day, I found someone to save.

I vaguely knew a woman who also drank heavily. She often slurred her words, and once I'd seen her break a glass and then crawl on her hands and knees through the jagged fragments to clean it up. I was terribly worried about her and called the local Council on Alcoholism to ask them for advice on how to help her.

They told me to be honest with her, to tell her that I was concerned about her drinking, and that I'd found out about ways she could get help. I did that, and even offered to quit drinking along with her, since it was "beginning" to get a little out of hand for me too. Together, I fantasized, we'd help each other find a brand-new sober life.

The weekend before our first appointment, I told my closest friend that I had decided to quit drinking. I told her that I had quit drinking once before and had turned into a boring, cliché-spouting robot, and that the same thing would happen again. I apologized for having to undergo a drastic personality change. I told her she would just have to accept that this was good-bye. She seemed puzzled, but did not contradict me, and we went off for one last drunken talk.

I showed up at the appointment with an incredible hangover and a passive acceptance of my fate.

Another Attempt at Recovery

It was just as I remembered it from before. All sorts of chipper people into recovery, full of cheer and self-confidence. They told us about meetings, gave us pamphlets, and set up counseling appointments. Once again, I was polite and com-pliant. I knew my friend needed my support and that I was tired of being hungover every morning. I remembered enough about AA from seven years before to believe that I was an old hand at this, so I settled into the routine almost gratefully. I decided to do what they told me so that I would feel better.

I stayed sober a little less than a month. I read the Big Book and went to meetings and counseling. I had a lot to say at AA meetings because I read all the literature and "knew" what the keys to recovery were. I was eager to help my counselor understand my complicated personality so that she could fig-ure out what was really wrong with me.

To my dismay, my friend was less willing than me to play the role of "recovering person." I found out she'd been drink-ing, and I was furious. I avoided her completely. If she wanted to crawl around in cut glass the rest of her life, fine, but I was going to make something of my life.

Except that I couldn't. Simply not drinking was possible, at least for a few weeks, and clearly I was feeling much better physically. But I was in emotional and psychological chaos. After a week or so, the numbness of going through the motions wore off, and so did the newness of waking up feeling vaguely okay. My life was still there, as confusing, threatening, and foreboding as ever. And *I* was still there, an empty shell spouting AA slogans, with a chaotic bunch of feelings and fears jumping around inside of me.

One night I thought I was going to explode. I marched to a liquor store, bought a six-pack of beer and said, Damn it, I don't care if I'm an alcoholic, I'd rather die drunk than live like this. The next day, I felt foolish. It struck me that a six-pack of beer was pretty feeble, and maybe I had overreacted a little. But off and on, for a couple of weeks, I'd drink — not my usual amounts, but enough to take the edge off. And all the while I kept going to meetings, sharing my insights on how to work the program, and going to counseling to help my counselor figure me out.

Hitting Bottom

Then, I had another chance to help someone else. A colleague, who lived in another state, was giving me a ride to a conference we were both scheduled to attend. He and I had met at other conferences and had really connected, seeing ourselves as sensitive, poetic spirits at odds with an abrasive and hostile modern world. And we both drank like fish. Here was my chance to share my "new way of life" and save him. I spent the eight hours traveling to the conference telling him about how wonderful sobriety was.

When we arrived at the hotel, we ran into a mutual friend who offered to buy us a drink. We sat down, and while thinking consciously of grapefruit juice, I ordered a glass of white wine. Then another, then a third, and then the bar closed. I went up to my room feeling triumphant; I had stopped at three.

The next night I decided to drink Manhattans, which I had been craving for weeks. I lost count of how many I had, but I eventually took my leave and stumbled up to my hotel room. I began to throw up all over the rug and the bed, unable to hold my head up over the wastebasket or even crawl to the bathroom.

Sometime near dawn, huddled in the corner of that hotel room, I accepted that I was an alcoholic, that I was powerless over alcohol, and that I knew nothing about sobriety. It was then that I became willing to surrender to a Power greater that myself.

I finally realized that alcohol is stronger than me. It is also stronger than the little bits of knowledge I picked up so easily in readings and at meetings. I realized that recovery was not something I could "just learn" the way I learned everything else; it was something that had to be lived.

In order to live, I had to surrender to my alcoholism and to the terms of recovery. I realized that my will could only carry me to a place where I was able to receive the help I needed. From there, I needed to take it on faith, to trust in the program and the words of other recovering people. If I didn't, I was lost and I'd keep repeating the same self-destructive patterns that now were clearly out of control.

It was then that I started on a path that has taken me here, to a typewriter on a sunny afternoon, seven years later, hoping that I can find the words to tell you about my journey. I tell you about myself not because my story is unique, not to save you or teach you, but to share my understanding of recovery as a healing journey, just as others have shared with me.

CHAPTER THREE

The First Steps

When I got home, I was drained, for the moment, of the self-will and false pride that had driven me to talk at AA meetings, criticize the literature, and "help" my counselor. I now clung to a few simple statements — don't drink, go to meetings, it will get better. When I saw my counselor, I was quiet, and scared. For the first time, I let her ask me questions. I tried, and often failed, to find words to answer her. I believed that whatever I could say would be a distortion, a smoke screen. I didn't trust myself. I had spent all of my life pretending to be someone else, and that someone got drunk when she didn't want to. I did not know how to be this new me, who was helpless, frightened, and in need.

A Meeting a Day

By talking with my counselor and going to AA meetings, I learned to let myself be helped. I didn't always understand what people were telling me, but the essence seemed to be that my feelings were normal and were part of the recovery process.

I had taken the First Step — I had admitted, deep down, that I was *powerless*, and that *my life had become unmanageable*. I had also begun to take the Second Step — believing that *a Power greater than myself could restore me to sanity*. God was mentioned fairly often in meetings. I had long ago decided that what was called God was an easy way out — a comfort for people too weak to face up to "real life." But during my last drunk, I discovered that alone I was weak and could not handle "real life" without alcohol.

19

Somewhere, outside myself, was a Power that could make it possible for me to recover and heal. It had worked for others, and most of them called this power God. I wasn't ready for that, but I did find a phrase I liked in the Big Book — "the sunlight of the spirit" — and decided that I could believe in a spirit that pervaded the world, a spirit from which I had been blocked by my drinking. The proof of its power was the people who had drunk like me, quit, and become loving and giving again. The sign of this Power's grace was that I could, for brief moments, glimpse what it was like to be happy and whole.

So, in those early months, I listened and followed. I went to an AA meeting every day. It seemed a haven, a place full of people who knew me and cared for me. The hubbub of conversation, the smell of the coffee, the crowded, smoky rooms were secure and reassuring. We began each meeting with the Serenity Prayer and spent the hour talking about how we were learning to live without drinking. Noon meetings became the center of my day. In them I could relax, expand, take comfort in the company of others who knew where I'd been, what had happened to me, and what it was like for me now. As we left to rejoin the world, I always felt sad. The meetings were so vibrant and intense that the rest of my day seemed drab and numb in comparison. I was still, even in sobriety, leading a double life.

No Virtue in Misery

How had these meetings, which I once thought were boring and cliché-ridden, come to mean so much to me? Besides the stunning level of honesty, of trust and affection, I was struck by how many of my fellow AA's had transcended tragedy in their lives. As I listened to them speak, my self-created tragic vision became a pale shadow of the real experiences they had lived through and learned to accept. What seemed like clichés to me were actually working in their lives. The slogans had, for them, taken on meanings deeper and more mysterious than anything I'd read or come up with myself.

I began to understand that true courage was accepting the pain in the world, and living fully and well through it. It is easy to describe and bemoan what is unfair, painful, cruel, and absurd in the world. To transcend it, to find meaning and joy in a life that goes beyond the tragic is a triumph. The men and women I saw in my group were accomplishing the miracle of transcendence — a miracle that eluded many of the suffering artists I had so long admired.

I began to realize that my fascination with the tortured, dark, and dramatic in life was a way to glamorize my self-created pain. No wonder I felt connected to those writers, singers, and painters who were suffering. No wonder they seemed to speak to me alone. No wonder I believed, for years and years, that only they could understand me.

By listening to recovering addicts, people who had learned how to walk through their own suffering, I began to see that there is no intrinsic honor in being a victim, no real courage in bemoaning fate, no automatic virtue in misery. The honor is in action, the courage in acceptance, the virtue in living with and through the real tragedies that exist in this world.

That realization helped me let go of my identification with the dark and painful vision of life as an abyss. It was not easy for me to give up the tortured poets and writers, the music of helplessness and despair, the endless hours of existential misery that I had called mine for so long. The writing, music, and misery seemed to be an integral part of my "real self." But I did give them up. I had to. They confirmed my pain, but never offered me a way out of it.

Now, after traveling the recovery journey longer, I realize that I can still appreciate different aspects of that world without getting swamped by them. As I've become more committed to ways of living that encourage openness, faith, and honesty, I can acknowledge and accept the validity of the experiences and beliefs of my former role models. They keep me connected to a pain that was once an important part of my life, a pain that many people cannot get beyond. They also help me see how far I've come and allow me to feel tremendous gratitude. But early in my recovery, I had to give them up completely — I wanted and needed to spend time only with other recovering people. They had become the only people who truly understood me.

Spiritual Boot Camp

For the first year or so of sobriety, my life was a series of meetings, where I shared the doubts, surprises, and setbacks of early recovery with people I came to love and trust. I needed them to give me the balance that helped me make it through each day without drinking.

I had not been through a treatment program, although many of my AA friends had. They would often use another language, a kind of psychological jargon that irritated me. I mistrusted it, and instead stuck close to the Big Book, the *Twelve Steps and Twelve Traditions*, other AA-approved literature, and old-timers who talked only the basics of AA. I found a sponsor who believed in working and reworking the Steps, and I followed her lead. My first year of recovery was spent in a diligent and increasingly narrowing quest for a time when I would be rewarded for all my hard work by suddenly becoming "happy, joyous, and free."

And yet I began to feel increasingly confined. Yes, I was staying sober, but my sobriety was becoming rigid and grim, a kind of relentless trudge through the Steps, to the meetings, through the Big Book, with the reward of the Promises dangling ahead of me, if I only learned to work the program "right."

I can look at myself back then and smile, recognizing a part of myself I still battle with: the grim and relentless taskmaster who follows rules and believes that I should discipline myself into happiness, and who also believes that if I am *very* good and work *really* hard, I will be rewarded. But at the time, I knew only that I was getting closer and closer to taking a drink, because the signs were all there: self-pity, resentment, the judgmental attitude, and loss of the spontaneity and ease that had been the gifts of early sobriety.

I longed for freedom, an escape from the bondage of the self, but I was again trapped, this time by my self-created AA rules.

I was using the AA program as a kind of recovery boot camp, a way to discipline myself into "fit spiritual condition." I used as my models other hard-liners: men and women who went to a meeting every day, read the Big Book, worked the Steps, and kept the plug in the jug. Like me, they had learned the Big Book by heart, and could find a passage in it for every occasion. They were sober, I was sober, and that was that. But it wasn't enough for me. "Pack all you can into the stream of life" the Big Book says — but what I was packing into my sobriety were rigid rules and strict self-discipline.

I knew something was amiss, and I began to look around for recovering people who seemed happy and free, who had the elusive generosity of spirit that mattered so much to me. I began a search for people who could laugh and cry, who would share how they were feeling, who had the spontaneity, energy, and freedom that I so longed for.

CHAPTER FOUR

People Like Me

It was through exploring and sharing feelings that I finally discovered the precious healing power of sobriety. When I opened myself to others, I found ways to make recovery a joyful, caring process. As I listened to people, instead of labeling them, I learned how to put into practice the principles I learned in meetings and the insights I gained in counseling. They showed me how working my program was more than a grim process of working the Steps, quoting the Big Book, and keeping the plug in the jug.

Until I acknowledged my feelings, I had been learning from others only by watching what they did, doing it too, and then hoping that I would be magically transformed. In many ways, I *had* changed. I had learned how not to take the first drink, how to live One Day at a Time, and how to believe in a Power greater than myself. I had also been learning, in counseling, that I held beliefs about myself and the world that were harmful to me, that were blocking me from a full and happy life. But somehow the ability to use my new knowledge to grow and to change was still missing. I felt stuck, afraid to go backward, afraid to keep going. I wanted something more, something I couldn't yet put into words.

At first I was frightened by this desire. Who was I to ask for this inexpressible "something more"? I knew alcohol was cunning, baffling, and powerful, and I was afraid that getting involved with anything other than "conference approved" thinking would lead me back to drinking. I was also afraid of losing my way, afraid of what would happen if I trusted my intuition and followed my heart in recovery.

In those meetings where sharing my feelings was as important as interpreting the Steps, I spent a lot of energy translating everything I heard back into program language. I wanted to make sure I wasn't being misled. What I found was that, while it wasn't always easy, it was possible to see how the principles of Twelve Step living were the common ground group members shared. Even if the language wasn't straight out of the Big Book, even if we were speaking from our hearts and not our heads, and even if our hearts were full of contradictions, this was recovery, this was healing, this was working the program.

No Longer Trying to Be a "Good AA"

I relaxed a little and realized how much more natural and comfortable it was to talk about my feelings and doubts with other people in my own words instead of only the phrases I heard in meetings. We were speaking to each other as fellow travelers and as friends, not merely trying to toe the line, walk the walk, or be "good AA's." It was such a relief.

I also began to realize that, for me, recovery involved coming to terms with myself not just as an alcoholic, but also as a recovering woman. AA opens the door and lays the foundation, but because of its early history, AA's core literature is from a male perspective. As a woman, I learned to read the "he" in the Big Book as if it were meant for me, but it was often a stretch.

Being a Woman in AA

In trying to be what I thought was a "good AA," I tried hard *not* to be a woman, to be instead a kind of neuter comrade. Sometimes being a woman got in the way, especially in the back to basics meetings I chose. Some of the old-timers seemed to think it was kind of cute for a "girl" like me to be an alcoholic. Some of the recovering men still kept some of their old ways, hustling the new women with the same tactics they used in bars. In spite of the common bond of alcoholism that we shared, I felt a discomfort in those meetings with topics like sex, love, and marriage, with issues from childhood, and with the host of jostling, confusing, tentative emotions that were beginning to surface in me.

I was feeling angry and confused about how complicated it was to be myself and be female, and I was struggling for ways to deal with it. I knew I looked down on the giggling, flirtatious women around me, even as I longed to be like them. I knew that I rebelled against the men in my life who wanted me to be docile and pliable, even as I tried to please them. Whoever I was becoming in sobriety was tender and terrified, and there were times when I felt especially vulnerable to authority, power, and the judgments of men.

I don't think there is a special, separate category of women's issues in recovery. Whatever characteristics alcoholics have are always connected to the basic issues of addiction. But because I'm a woman, sometimes I'll approach the issues differently, or see them in different ways. We are living in a time when gender roles are in flux. I often feel that I have to make it all up as I go along. Then, I especially need the help of other recovering women — I feel safer, more able to risk and share myself. I've come to need trust, warmth, compassion, and empathy from other women as I continue to learn what my feelings are and who I am. Growing numbers of recovering men have been sharing similar needs and concerns with each other. Whether in gender-specific support groups or in mixed AA meetings, the need for openness and the affirmation of feelings has become essential for me.

The Voice of the Heart

I've belonged to recovery groups that were different from each other, and I was different in each of them. What I've learned, I've often learned haphazardly and piecemeal, re-membering and forgetting, picking up and letting go. Different issues troubled me, different ties bound me, different traits needed to be recognized and addressed. But always there was healing for me in the warmth and closeness of the groups where we shared things that none of us really understood or accepted, until we had the chance to express them to each other.

These issues, ties, and traits seem, when I write about them now, to be incredibly simple and obvious. They are all *living problems*, things that emerge as we learn to live sober. Yet no matter how simple, obvious, and familiar they have become, I still can lose my way and get caught up in my old ways of thinking about myself.

Recovery, for me, is not a straight line or a narrow path. It is an ongoing, upward spiral. I don't finish with anything; I just learn to pass through it more quickly and less painfully. Old ways become less comfortable; new ways become more liberating. What I've learned in recovery, and what I offer here, are not simple answers or hard-and-fast rules or quick and easy shortcuts to happiness. They are ways I've used to define who I am, ways that give me the strength and freedom to be myself.

We've all developed defenses and distorted ways of understanding ourselves and others, both when we were children and while we drank. These defense systems and distortions continue to haunt many of us — ghost selves from the past, ghost voices that keep us trapped and blocked.

For me, the journey of recovery has been a journey through a crowd of selves I thought I was, or thought I ought to be, a journey through a din of voices telling me what I should and should not feel. The miracle of recovery is that we have the possibility for the first time in our life to choose our own voice and speak from the heart.

PART II

HEALING WOUNDS

Once we are freed from acting out our addiction, we are still trapped by the feelings, beliefs, and patterns we learned in and through our disease. We may find ourselves overwhelmed by things we were once able to stifle, avoid, or deny. Our old ways of living have wounded us, and they can continue to harm us in our sobriety. We need to find ways to recognize and heal the wounds of addiction.

CHAPTER FIVE

Selves and Voices

In my thirty years of wanting to be perfect, I collected a crowd of phantom selves — people I wanted to be, thought I was supposed to be, or was treated as. I was better at being some of them than others. What they had in common was that they were roles, parts of myself that never quite came together.

I would draw on different selves, depending on who I was with, what situation I was in, or how I wanted to be perceived. There was the *adorable little girl*, sweet, docile, loved by parents and teachers. There was the *brazen barmaid*, slinging drinks and fending off passes. There was the *brilliant student*, aglow with a desire to speak out and learn; and the *tortured poet*, clogged with pain and half-formed words; the *sensuous woman*, erotic and powerful; the *martyr-rescuer*, helping anyone who had lost his or her way; and, finally, the *competent professional*, efficient and successful. Had I been married, with children, I'm sure I would have added two more: the *ever-understanding mother*, and the *perfect, loving wife*.

Being My Selves

All these were, in some ways, real parts of me. But they never agreed. Instead, they would crowd around me, clamoring to be heard. Bringing one to the fore would set the others off grumbling. I lived with a constant sense of noise and incompleteness. It was hard to be just one of them. It was even harder to figure out which one was the one that would "work," that would get people to like me so I could like myself.

31

What was even more confusing was that each self had a lot to say, often in contradiction to the other selves. The adorable little girl said that I should always be sweet and innocent, never angry or moody. The brazen barmaid said I should give as good as I got, never get stepped on, taken advantage of, or hurt. The brilliant student said I should always be reading and thinking, never get bored, have fun, or take time off. The sensuous woman said I should be spontaneous and sexy. The martyr-rescuer said no sacrifice was too great if it helped people. The competent professional said that feelings got in the way of performance, that all duties had to be fulfilled completely and perfectly.

Try as I might, it was impossible to please all the voices at once. So, I found ways to live with only one or a few of them at a time. One of the tricks I devised was to subdivide — not let people know me well enough to see more than a few of my roles. I divided my life and my friends so that each of them knew different, and relatively compatible, sides of me. I lived in fear of being in a situation where I'd be found out. How would I know who to be if I saw students of mine while I was with my boyfriend in the bar where I worked?

Figuring out how to negotiate a public life was difficult, but living with myself was virtually impossible. F. Scott Fitzgerald, who spent his last years trying to quit drinking, called 3:00 A.M. "the dark night of the soul." It was late at night that it would all come crashing down on me: the different selves, the voices telling me to be different things. I silenced some only to be overcome by others. I would lie in bed in the dark with my heart pounding, not knowing who to be or if there was anything left of something I could call the real me. It seemed the only way out was to make up another list of "shoulds," a new role that would combine the "best" and eliminate the "worst" of all the voices.

Trying to Find My Voice

I lived in a world of dos and don'ts when I was drinking, and most of them stayed with me after I quit. It wasn't until I heard other recovering people talk about those same rules that

I realized how destructive they were. They seemed especially harmful to women struggling with contradictory messages — that we should always be warm and loving, but never angry or selfish; always assertive, but never a doormat; always pure and innocent, but never rejecting; always attractive, but never seductive; always in control of our feelings, but never domineering or bossy . . . we were all trying to be some of these things just long enough to feel good about ourselves.

Every so often one of us would come up for air and wail, "Where are the rules?" We wanted rules to follow so we could be happy. I think that's why self-help books, the simpler the better, sell so well. They lay out a way to be that seems clear, concise, and unambiguous. It's a relief to think, *Ah! Now I've got it. If I just follow this path, all will be well.* Dieting and exercise can be such regimens — a set of conditions that, if met, lets us feel good about ourselves. That's why it was so easy for me to misuse the Twelve Step program; it became a regimen. I made a list of shoulds and musts that left me feeling resentful, trapped, and rebellious.

It is the contingency principle: If I do x, y, and z, then I am a good person; if I do not, then I am a bad person. But how to choose among my contradictory voices? They make such different demands, involve so many mutually exclusive things. It was a no-win situation, and in the years I drank, I tried and failed to come up with a simple set of guidelines that would let me like myself.

Sorting Through My Feelings

Recovery operates on a different basis. We are not bad people trying to be good, but sick people trying to get well. We are good people trying to learn how to act and feel better. We are trying to feel a deep acceptance and love for who we are.

Many people in early recovery develop a set of defenses to channel and control emotions they have come to see as wrong, ugly, or too demanding. We may go numb when we feel resentment, fear, or jealousy, while good feelings, such as caring and joy, are okay and allowed expression. Our confusion is compounded by some program advice, which seems to suggest that negative feelings like anger are possible preludes to relapse.

Some emotional states were so familiar to us that they felt like old friends. Shame was one of these. We could don it at a moment's notice. During our drinking years, we developed ways to keep what we saw as dangerous emotions under control, only to slip into other states like shame or anxiety. We did this without being completely aware of it. What we called self-pity might really have been sadness. Instead of allowing ourselves to be sad, we shamed ourselves, saying things like, *What do I have to be sad about? There are a lot of people worse off than I am.*

Feelings, in the end, are at the center of my recovery. That I have them, that they are easy to mislabel, that I can learn not to beat myself up about them, and that it's okay to express these feelings openly is what I've begun to learn. Listening to myself as I spill out the combination of emotions, labels, judgments, and apologies helps me hear what I am doing to myself and how I am setting myself up to feel rotten. It is the contingency principle again: if I feel and act a certain way, then I'm okay; if not, then I'm a wretched human being.

It is not an easy pattern to break. Many of us have been at it a long time. Besides, we often wondered what would happen if we ever let up on ourselves. If we simply were ourselves and just felt our feelings, wouldn't we be out of control, swinging between rage and tears? Wouldn't we become hideous, rotten people, once all the deep-down garbage came to the surface? How would we get anything done if we let up on ourselves? Wouldn't we turn into lumps sitting there, just glad to be ourselves?

Many of us thought feelings had terrible power, that they could leap out of nowhere and take over. We thought they had to be squelched, coddled, and translated so that they wouldn't overwhelm us and everyone else around us. This is, in AA terminology, a form of false pride, a grandiose belief in our own power to influence the workings of the world.

It sounds a little silly now, but it really seemed that emotions were dangerous when I was in the full throes of my addiction.

Most of the people I know in recovery have had terrible experiences with emotions. For them, emotions *did* seem to come out of nowhere; they *had* affected others when they let loose with tears and rage. Emotions had become unpredictable and dangerous, especially when we were drinking.

What we begin to learn, just by being sober, is that we don't have to live in constant fear of losing our mind. We don't need to keep such a tight rein on our feelings. In sobriety, our feelings can still seem confusing and scary, but they don't have to erupt and destroy everything. When we're sober, we can know and trust our feelings as part of ourselves.

Even in recovery, feelings may come out jumbled and incoherent, but we are discovering that they aren't inherently alien or evil. Our emotions can signal our basic human desire for love, connection, and acceptance, even if they seemed like something else. We had stuffed our feelings for so long that we thought they had turned into something repulsive. But once we got them into the light, we saw that they were just your garden variety human feelings. They weren't "down there" waiting to leap out; they were just there, waiting to be listened to.

Breaking My Spell of Numbness

We can feel more alive, more true to ourselves, when we express our feelings. Surprisingly, people don't hide their face in horror, collapse in a heap, or rush out of the room in terror when we say what we feel. Instead, we find trust and affection for each other when we express our very real, very ordinary emotions. We learn to see ourselves in each other and love the selves we find.

For me, really opening up took a long time. Oh, I talked. I always do when I'm nervous — a helpful chatter designed to make people feel at ease and to show them how much I identified with them. But the whole thing began to be silly — what was the point of chattering on about abstract feelings when they were really there, and scary.

I don't remember what set me off, what horrible feeling I revealed, sniffling into my Kleenex, apologizing for being so weak and taking up so much of the group's time. But whatever it was, it broke a spell I had lived under for a long time.

The results overwhelmed me. The people who up until then I had thought of as friends told me how distant I had seemed. Some said they had even been put off by how "together" I appeared. Now they were relieved, and they felt a genuine affection for me. I was someone like them after all. And now we could learn how to trust each other.

It was an amazing revelation for me, that my attempts to be "close" through close, analytical listening and wise words were really a way to put up a wall between myself and others. These defenses kept others from knowing me, and kept me from knowing myself. They kept me locked away in a place that was empty and lonely, even though it looked pretty good from the outside.

For me, opening up about my feelings was a kind of meltdown process, where my defenses were gradually melted away. I began to relax and bask in the acceptance that was possible as I revealed what I had been so afraid of — myself.

It took a lot of listening, watching, and taking risks for me to see how groundless my fears were, and to find out how liberating it was to let go of them. I want to share with you the kinds of things I learned about feelings, and what it has been like to begin to accept them, even embrace them as tools for growth.

We are capable of many different emotions, and I balk at limiting our complex range of feelings by trying to list them all. But the issues that kept giving me, and the people around me, the most trouble were: *anger, shame, fear,* and *grief.*

CHAPTER SIX

The Faces of Anger

For me, anger was the most confusing and frightening emotion. Learning how to let myself feel it, and express it, taught me a lot about other emotions. Maybe anger offered me the biggest challenge because it is so undeniable, so strong, and often labeled inappropriate for women. As I learned to recognize, experience, express, and let go of anger, I learned how to label, share, and make peace with other feelings that confused and troubled me.

Even more than my other feelings, anger disguises itself immediately. I grew up believing that there is no excuse for anger, that any upsetting situation should be examined, explained, and calmly rationalized away. If someone did something to hurt me, I quickly assumed that the person was not really at fault. I tried to understand and empathize with the person, telling myself there was something wrong with me for being mad.

If I was waiting in line at the grocery store and the clerk was dawdling away while the time on my parking meter ran out, I would be angry inside. But I would also tell myself, *It doesn't really matter. There's nothing you can do about it. Everybody does things at their own pace.* Anger at *people* would immediately turn into an elaborate acceptance of their right to do anything at all. Now that sounds mighty serene, doesn't it? Very saintly. As a matter of fact, very much like a martyr.

Anger at *things* was a different story. I often didn't even know I was angry. I instantly blamed myself for my reactions to situations such as my car breaking down, a traffic jam, or a bureaucratic foul-up. I told myself that I should overcome and accept anything that happens in the world. I believed it was my fault if I got upset, that it was my attitude that had to change.

Caring Enough to Get Angry

The confusing thing about anger and alcoholism recovery is that the Big Book says anger is a luxury we cannot afford and that it will get us drunk. Yet, my old ways of stuffing anger, of trying to rationalize it away, felt dishonest. I was telling myself that I was calm and accepting when actually I was furious. I said in an AA meeting once that I didn't practice the HALT program (never get too Hungry, Angry, Lonely, or Tired) but the HILT program, because I didn't get angry, just indignant. I could get a little huffy, or sometimes even hostile, but angry? No way. There was no excuse for it.

Well. One of the things I've found out is that anger is natural when things happen in our lives that are unfair, senseless, cruel, or constraining. Anger simply *is*, and we can feel it and express it without the world coming to an end. Role playing helped me with this. I would practice saying, "That's not fair!" Or, "I'm really mad!" At first, I would whisper it. Then, I would gradually work up enough steam to say it like I meant it, because, of course, I did.

I also began to remember the times when friends clearly and directly expressed their anger to me. I was upset, but it usually cleared the air and relieved the tension between us. When my friends saw how my drinking was destroying me and furiously told me just how fed up they really were, they were showing me that they cared. They cared enough about me *to* get angry. They wanted me to know how they felt — frustrated and helpless. And they knew how to tell me — directly and honestly.

I believe now that feelings expressed clearly and consistently are clear, consistent connections to our inner self and to other people. Recognizing and expressing anger can mean, *I matter and you matter. Here's what's going on with me; I want you to know.* When we acknowledge and respect our feelings and express ourselves clearly to those around us, we cleanse and heal ourselves.

What I used to offer were expressions of anger that don't cleanse or heal — cold resentment, nasty hostility, or huffy snideness. These are corrosive expressions of anger that come from trying to pretend that I'm not really mad at all. They poison me and poison other people because they are

- dishonest — they don't acknowledge the anger,
- indirectly expressed — by sniping, glaring, or sarcasm, and
- never resolved — they just sit there and fester.

Maybe these indirect and corrosive expressions of anger are what the Big Book means when it warns us about the incompatibility of anger and sobriety.

I began to see that there was nothing wrong with feeling angry or with expressing anger. But the trick is to label anger appropriately, and then to express myself clearly and directly. I believe now that I and the people I am angry with are better off when I am honest about my feelings.

The Harm Resentment Was Causing Me

Anger has another face — resentment — which is rage from the past that we won't let go of. Resentments have torn us up. Many of us have really tried to work the Steps, make our amends, and do a daily inventory, but we've not been able to eliminate our need to hang on to our rage over things that happened to us in the past.

We have been angry about a lot of things, although it took us a while to realize it. First, we may have been angry at being alcoholics. Why do we have to work so damn hard to recover while "normal" people seem to waltz through life doing whatever they please? We may have been angry at ourselves because we kept on drinking even after we *knew* it was destroying us. Why did we take so long to get help?

And we were probably angry at people in our past — at relationships we clung to long after they turned sour, at those who used us and hurt us, at our parents who shaped us. These were our ghosts, including all the people who got tangled up in our lives while we were tangled up in our addiction.

So how do we learn to let go of those resentments that seem to run so deep? For me, letting go began with realizing that other people had resentments, too, and that mine were doing me damage. I saw how much energy they were taking, how my buried rage at alcoholism, lovers, parents, and myself was eating me alive. I saw, too, how resentments were blocking me from the present, from being able to live my life moment by moment. Resentments kept the past present, forcing me to remain trapped by my addiction.

To free myself, I learned to recognize my resentment for what it was — anger. I learned to accept that part of myself and then to express my needs directly to the person with whom I was angry. If that person wasn't available, I could acknowledge my feelings with friends or in a support group. Only then was I able to let go of it. I got better and better at recognizing resentment, at recognizing when I was *re*-feeling old anger and keeping myself trapped. When I brought these insights back to the Steps, my program made more sense where resentment was concerned. I could release my anger to my Higher Power with the Sixth and Seventh Steps, and I could remain free of grounds for new resentments by working the Tenth Step on a daily basis.*

Silencing the "Tyrant in My Head"

Anger at ourselves is a special brand of anger. With me it often takes the form of self-hate. To be healthily angry at myself, to tell myself I'm angry and then let go of it, is a skill I have yet to master. Instead, I'm learning how to be patient with myself, to be loving and accepting, and to treat myself as young, inexperienced, well-meaning, and recovering.

---

* Editor's note: The Twelve Steps of Alcoholics Anonymous appear at the back of this book, page 101.

My self-hate is still surprisingly hard to recognize. I've found that it often masquerades as depression, exhaustion, perfectionism, or rigid self-discipline.

In counseling and in group sessions, people seem to pick up on it right away. They'll say, "You're being a little hard on yourself, don't you think?" Or, "Sounds like you're a little angry with yourself right now." It always stops me short. They are usually right. What I think I'm doing is problem-solving, trying to find what's wrong with me and what needs to be "fixed."

I think we alcoholics have spent so long berating ourselves that, when we get sober, we go right on trying to "fix" ourselves with self-discipline. We continue to list shoulds and shouldn'ts, we institute new regimens, and then we get angry at ourselves for not living up to our unrealistic expectations. We get angry at ourselves for not turning into perfect people overnight.

Again and again I hear myself and others in the program say, "But I should know better by now. I've been sober all this time!" as if somewhere there is a ladder of sobriety, and we're a few rungs off from where we should be. That is the way I was misusing the AA program. I was telling myself that I should be different. I was trying to work the Steps so I would be magically, immediately transformed. I wanted to become a "good AA" because I hated who I seemed to be.

I still have what I call the "tyrant in my head" — a little drill sergeant who tells me to toe the mark, walk the line, and who gets furious at the seemingly bumbling, inept, lazy self that refuses to fall into step. But what I'm learning now is that the bumbling, inept, and lazy self is really a *response* to the little tyrant — a way I learned while I was drinking to keep true to my real needs and desires.

Enjoying My Bumbling Self

My bumbling self can be a lot nicer to be around when she ignores the tyrant and says, quietly, "I'll do it my way, thank you." When she *does* listen to the tyrannical voice, she gets whiny and full of self-pity. The combination of self-hate and self-pity feels lousy and can easily turn into paralyzing anxiety or depression. My bumbling self is not really all that lazy or inept. With a little love and attention, a little patience and acceptance, she gets along just fine.

It is as if we have inside of us a child who has been ignored, lectured to, denied, and hated. But he or she is a little child who we can learn to listen to and love. Much of what I've learned about my feelings I've learned from her. She's the one who aches, gets scared and angry. She's who I've tried to silence, and yet have longed to let speak. She's who I need to learn to love.

Chuckles

I've had plenty of times in recovery when I've been depressed or felt too tired to do anything but mope around. Almost automatically, I start planning a grueling new low-calorie, high-exercise regimen of all work and no play. That's when my serenity goes out the window. Eventually, I end up feeling even more worthless and exhausted and unlovable.

If I stop and listen to what I'm telling myself, it is usually a litany of shoulds — that I *should* be happy and energetic and productive and serene and thin and organized and on top of everything. And that's just for starters. Meanwhile, I'm also telling myself that I am the opposite of all those things — that I'm miserable and sick and stupid and impatient and hateful and lazy and anxious and fat and my life is a mess. At best.

What I'm learning to do, once I recognize the little tyrant voice with its impossible expectations and incredibly harsh judgment, is ... chuckle. Now I know that may sound strange, but I learned it from hours of hearing myself go on and on, weeping, shredding my Kleenex, and hearing friends suggest that maybe, just maybe, I was being a little extreme. A chuckle, a little laugh, like a hint of sun breaking through the clouds, lifts the spell and makes the little tyrant sound ridiculous. I think it is the little girl inside of me, stubborn, resilient, and spunky, who remembers how to laugh.

I once escaped a week-long bout with self-hate when I noticed my sorry-looking geranium in the window. I asked myself how anybody as revolting as I thought myself to be could keep and love such a dopey-looking flower? It somehow broke the spell of self-loathing; it let me laugh with my little girl, and it gave us both a break.

Laughter can release us from bondage to that self that we alcoholics create when we compulsively berate ourselves for not being perfect. The laughter comes from a self I'm growing fond of, a more lighthearted, spontaneous, unfinished self. A self that sobriety allows me to discover.

CHAPTER SEVEN

Shame and Guilt

Many psychologists believe that anger turned inward, or self-hate, usually has roots in shame. When I was drinking, shame was my constant companion. It was a chronic state, a snake that slithered its way through every aspect of my life. What did I have to feel so ashamed of? Everything.

Indicting Myself for Being Human

First off, I was a drunk. I had known for a long time that drinking was causing me problems, but I did it anyway. I didn't understand then that part of having the disease of alcoholism is to continue to drink even when we know we're destroying ourselves. I knew I was doing something that was hurting me, but I couldn't understand *why* I was doing it. I felt bad, ashamed.

Worse, I was really getting drunk. Not always sloppily, disgustingly drunk, but nonetheless regularly and thoroughly drunk. *Nice girls don't let that happen*, I said to myself. They don't get loud and obnoxious, or bore people, or throw up. They don't feel like death warmed over every morning. Nice girls are perky, organized, and charming. I wasn't and I felt ashamed.

But my shame wasn't limited to my drinking. If it had been tied only to that, I would have been shame-free when I finally quit. I *still* contend with shame and it can still pervade my life, if I let it. Shame became a habit that told me over and over how inadequate and how wrong I was. For much of my life, I wasn't comfortable with who I was, how I felt, or what I did, as if I was indicting myself for being human.

For me, shame was tied up with people-pleasing and perfectionism, with the impossible desire to be all things to all people. I wanted to be and I expected myself to be an ideal friend, a wonderful teacher, a thoughtful daughter, a loving wife, an all-around incredible woman. I still sometimes get caught on the treadmill of striving for perfection but always falling short, then feeling shameful and vowing to mend my ways, only to repeat the cycle.

Sound familiar? I'm playing out another version of my drinking behavior: a no-win situation where all I can see is what I've screwed up, and then all I see is what I need to do to cover it up. I'm vulnerable to shame, I think, because I'm so used to feeling rotten, and because part of me still believes that to become a decent human being, I have to mercilessly pound myself into shape.

I sometimes feel that I no longer have any excuse for less than a perfect performance. During the years I was drinking, I had a way out. Not a particularly comfortable way out, but handy: *If I hadn't been hungover, or drunk, I could have been more efficient, more understanding, more considerate, more of whatever I was supposed to be.* As long as I was caught up in alcoholism, I wasn't completely responsible for my actions; once I quit drinking, I was. I found this responsibility scary.

Setting Myself Up for Shame

Shame is personal, a sense of being a failure as a human being. Shame says I'm a bad *person.* Guilt is public and has to do with morality. Guilt says something I've *done* is bad.

Most of the guilt I felt when I first quit drinking was for past actions, for people I'd hurt, things I'd done and left undone. That's where the Eighth and Ninth Steps of the AA program — the amends process — made such a difference. Listing the people I harmed, and making amends to them, was a healing process. I've heard those Steps referred to as the "ground glass" Steps because they help us get rid of the ground glass in our system. Taking these Steps is a crucial beginning toward living an honest, straightforward life, one without deception.

But the Eighth and Ninth Steps were, for me, only a beginning. Like much in the AA program, I can interpret it so rigidly that I do myself harm. I sometimes lock myself into a cycle of self-punishment that blocks me from other people, and from the sunlight of the spirit that has been the gift of my sobriety. The Tenth Step — taking a personal inventory and promptly admitting when I'm wrong — can send me into a pit of self-loathing. I can *always* find areas where I've fallen short, even if I've done nothing wrong. My shame can cut so deeply that I sometimes rake myself over the coals for doing things that are perfectly human, reasonable, understandable, and easily forgiven, except by the tyrant in my head.

By talking with each other we can recognize how impossibly high, and contradictory, our expectations of ourselves sometimes are — and how alluring, familiar, and destructive shame can be. We want always to be compassionate, sensitive, understanding, and generous, while at the same time being assertive, successful, efficient, and productive. If we manage to be only one or two of those, we feel ashamed about falling short on the others. There is no end to the list of things we can come up with to feel rotten about — shame speaks from all our voices, all our selves, which jostle around trying to run our life.

As I realized how well I set myself up for shame, and how familiar it was to feel rotten, I also began to see how sobriety could turn guilt and shame into a new kind of problem. Now that I was sober, I felt that I ought to be living up to my old, high expectations. Drinking, the feeble justification I used all those years, no longer cut it. Worse, I had an image of sobriety that said I could be serene, competent, fulfilled, and loving, if I just . . .

Just what? This was reminiscent of those voices of the many selves I had created, selves I had thought I should become. Now, in recovery, I had added another, seemingly healthy self that said, *I ought to be serene and together, a perfect person now that I'm sober.* And so I found myself lacking once again, imperfect, flawed.

Rationally thinking through whether or not I "ought" to feel guilty didn't really help. Truthfully, there are no hard-and-fast rules about what is right and wrong in most everyday situations — right for whom? when? under what circumstances? What I found myself doing was reasoning my way out of feeling guilty, yet still feeling bad.

Discovering My Values

The child within, that stumbling, vulnerable inner self, can help us decipher what is truly right and wrong, good and bad, for us. As we learn who that child is, and what he or she wants, and as we affirm the truths we've discovered in recovery, we find a truer measure of what is right for us. As we discover ways to live congruently with our inner self, we find out what matters to us, what our values are. Those values can become our guideposts and teach us to see when we have truly done harm, and when we need to make amends. Our values can help us recognize our true transgressions and distinguish them from the host of shoulds we heap on ourselves.

Prayer and asking for the forgiveness of a Higher Power helps many of us. Prayer for me is the way I listen to the healing spirit within myself. When I am feeling guilty, I am learning to use my guilt to discover my own implicit beliefs, and to then decide, in concert with my inner spirit, what is right for me.

Guilt can be a guiding force, once it is distinguished from shame and examined with loving and patient attention. Both shame and guilt reveal to us our hidden rules, our beliefs. They bring them to the surface so that we can choose what truly matters. Guilt tells us we need to take responsibility for actions that are contrary to our values. Shame can tell us we need to take responsibility for our *re*actions that block us from the forgiveness of our Higher Power and the support of other people.

Letting Go of Old, Destructive Roles

Most of the shame I feel is tied up with destructive beliefs — my belief that I

- can and should control myself and all other people, places, and things within reach,
- should meet other people's expectations of me,
- am perfectible,
- should be "above" feelings, and
- can't know what's best for me.

When I don't control myself and others, when I don't meet other people's expectations of me, when I am flawed and imperfect, when I am awash in emotion, when I go against convention, when I act on intuition, I feel ashamed.

But I'm coming to believe that full recovery involves trusting my own rules, with the guidance of other recovering men and women and my Higher Power. Trusting my own rules means letting go of control, accepting my humanness, my imperfections, and learning how to act in ways that are in harmony with my vulnerable, intuitive self. Living like that is scary, and my sudden attacks of shame are frequent signs that I haven't let go of my old, destructive rules.

When I do let go of those rules, when I am open to the healing power of people who are learning to accept and celebrate themselves, and who are beginning to live in ways that express their authentic inner desires, I am free to do the same. I am learning to unravel the bonds of self-imposed rules and to escape the chronic shame of "not being what I'm supposed to be." I am learning how to live in self-caring ways.

Self-Respect Is Not Selfish

I have always been afraid that, deep down, I am a very selfish person. I feel incredible anxiety when I choose to do something only because it will give me — unworthy, imperfect me — pleasure. I have spent years trying to squelch the needy child in me who wants love, attention, and time to play. Whenever I heard how, in recovery, we learn "self care," I got uncomfortable. It sounded like a sneaky way to let yourself be selfish.

I could claim that quitting drinking wasn't really selfish, because it meant that I had more to give to others. And I could even convince myself that working on my recovery wasn't at all selfish for the very same reason. After all, the more I learned about myself and others, the better person I became, the more I could give, and the more I'd enhance the universe.

Well, that kind of thinking gets me into a real bind when I discover that I have things that I want to do just for me, like spend all day in bed reading, or staying up all night working, or taking a nap and then going for a walk. I discover, too, that there are people in the world who frazzle and drain me. There are situations that bore me silly or drive me up the wall. And then I feel ashamed, not only for being selfish, but also for being judgmental. Anyway, who am I to be so nice to myself? What have I done to deserve it? Besides, don't I owe the world, and everyone in it, my best self, my best effort, my total energy?

In recovery, I am learning that self-care is not cold, narcissistic insensitivity. It's not a sneaky way to be selfish. And self-care is not justifiable only as a prelude to selfless action. Consistent self-care is self-respect. It is caring enough about myself to treat myself well.

Self-Respect Does Not Have to Be Earned

The cruelest thing about perfectionism, and the rigid thinking that we alcoholics seem to have in common, is that they prevent us from loving ourselves as we are. We find it hard to respect ourselves. We often don't like ourselves very much. We *wait* to like ourselves and *delay* our own approval until some future time when we *deserve* it. We pummel ourselves with ought-tos and shoulds. We make pacts and deals: *I'll take a break when I've finished up all the things I have to do.* We set up meaningless contingencies: *I'll like myself when I lose ten pounds and exercise every day.* We deny ourselves things we want: *I don't really need it, do I?* We look down on those who love us as we are — *They don't know the real me yet.* Or, *They have no taste.*

What's going on here? Even when we're sober and doing everything we can to recover, why do we have such disrespect for ourselves?

Why am I capable of showing more love and acceptance of a stranger's dog than I am for myself? I wish I knew, but the issue for me these days is not why something exists, but what can I do about it? How can I learn to be gentle with myself, to love and care for myself, to treat myself with respect?

Self-respect is so basic, so fundamental to recovery that I think the lack of it connects with all the other feelings and beliefs that cause me so much trouble. Learning to respect and care for myself is at the core of my recovery. And I can't do it alone. When I'm left to my own devices, my old patterns and beliefs run rampant. But in the company of loving and accepting friends, and with the help of my Higher Power, I can tentatively, gently, try out new ways of respectfully defining myself.

At first, it was little things: enjoying a bubble bath, taking a nap, buying expensive face cream. Then, I began to try bigger, scarier self-caring things: saying no when I didn't want to do something. (Yikes!) Or, checking out my own needs and wants before making a decision. (Eeek!) Or, making plans to do exactly what I wanted to do, in spite of my old, relentless shoulds. (Aaaugh!)

Caring for Her-In-Me

Respecting myself means knowing myself, loving myself, and acting in my own best interest. This is terrifically difficult for me at every step. I wonder, *Do I really know myself? Can I really like myself with all my flaws? Are my own desires valid? Worthy? Acceptable?*

Yes again and again is what the chorus of recovering voices tell me. *Oh, no!* is what the chorus of selves in me answers to each question — except, of course, for that child I lost somewhere in the progression of this disease, a child who has always craved, and never gotten, the love and attention she longed for and deserves. On the verge of some self-caring action, when I am torn between the voices of recovery and the voices of addiction, she pipes up with a hopeful voice. "Please," she says. And if I please her, I am being true to myself. I am connecting with and caring for her-in-me. I am accepting and respecting my responsibility to myself.

CHAPTER EIGHT

The Faces of Fear

Acting in ways that are self-caring, letting go of my shoulds and oughts, becoming free of relentless, self-punishing shame, and accepting who I am without any *if onlys* or *except fors*, is frightening. In fact, almost every new phase of my recovery has terrified me: I wait for retribution, for a sudden, swift reprisal, for the rug to be pulled out from under my feet. I often feel a nameless, permeating dread.

Dread — or, Waiting for My Plane to Crash

It's as if I expect catastrophe to strike if I do what I want. Whenever I am on the verge of doing something good for myself, I become convinced that I have contracted a fatal ailment, will shortly be in a car wreck, or will not survive a plane ride. When something nice comes my way, some award, opportunity, or break, I become terrified. I wonder, *What's the trade-off? What bad thing will happen to balance it off?*

This expectation of catastrophic retribution, this feeling of imminent disaster if I do or receive good things, is something I share with many other recovering people. We seem to believe in some vengeful force that will hurl down punishment if we address our own needs, act in our own best interests, or are given good things.

When I feel this kind of dread, it tells me that I'm still judging myself as unworthy of good things. It tells me that I am probably about to do something that still feels unfamiliar: acting in my own best interests; living by my new, healthy rules; accepting what's good for me because I deserve it; repudiating the confining and corrosive beliefs that I used to live by.

I figure this kind of fear is okay. It will probably lessen as I fully accept my worthiness and the possibilities of recovery. This fear shows me the hold the past still has on me, but it also shows me the progress I'm making as a signal that I'm trying new things.

Anxiety — or, Terror of Everyday Life

When I was drinking, I was almost always anxious. I was anxious alone, and when I was around other people. I was afraid of losing control, saying something stupid, or looking foolish. If there was alcohol around, the chances were good that some of those things would happen. No matter how hard I tried to limit how much I drank, I turned into a blurry word machine, full of sentences I *had* to say. I was sulky and silent, until something set me off, or I was maudlin and confessional, telling strangers my life story. The next day, I was a mass of recrimination and self-doubt. I asked myself, *How could I have said that, acted that way, been such a fool?*

The fear of being, looking, and sounding foolish is a relatively simple fear, but it crippled me. Sometimes it became a devastating anxiety — a phobia. In my drinking days, I had periods of weeks or months when I would be afraid to leave the house, to go to work, shop, or do laundry. I would force myself to go out, and I'd be edgy and tense until I could get back home, where it was safe, where I could be alone. One summer, even forcing myself didn't work. I spent the summer drinking and reading novels. When it came time for classes to start, I broke my ankle, giving myself another six weeks at home, safe.

Sometimes the anxiety would seem to lift, and I'd go on about my business. Then, it would suddenly swoop down on me again, and I'd desperately try to find a place to hide. This general terror of everyday life lifted as I remained sober. (Free-floating anxiety is apparently fairly common among practicing alcoholics, and some experts think it may be alcohol-induced

— that there is a physiological basis for it.) I still get occasional attacks, but they are rare, and nothing compared to the way they used to be. These days, I feel anxiety mostly when I am feeling alone and insecure, and when I am about to meet strangers who I'm afraid might not like me.

Fear of Rejection — or, God Forbid I Should Look Foolish

I teach at a university, and it still can scare me to stand up in front of a class, not knowing for certain what will come out of my mouth, whether my slip is showing, or if I'll get through the hour making sense. But it doesn't terrify me like it used to.

I realize now that the worst that can happen is that I'll say something stupid and look stupid doing it, and if that happens I can always say something like "Sheesh, I'm sorry for not making sense, but the point is that I have these things I want you to understand, so please bear with me." I've realized that other people aren't the enemy. They aren't cruel and vicious, always ready to strike. The addict in me believed that, and I projected that belief onto others when I was drinking.

Like most people, I am always a little scared before I enter a room full of strangers. I want to have myself "all put together." I feel vulnerable when I am in situations where attention is on me and I haven't had hours to practice and prepare. But the addict in me makes this fear deeper than normal — I don't *ever* want to look foolish because I'm afraid of being ridiculed.

My fear of looking foolish comes from a fear of being judged. This fear runs rampant when I am being judgmental — the two seem tied together. As I learn to accept others for themselves, I grow less frightened of what other people might think of me. As I learn to be forgiving and understanding of others, I learn to be forgiving and understanding of myself. As I accept myself, I am more free of the fear of others not accepting me.

What's nice about all this is that I can now meet people on common ground. I'm not hiding from them, or presenting a false self, or pulling off some pretense of perfection. I'm just there, with them. We're on the same side, looking out into the world, rather than facing off and sizing each other up. This commonality and honesty give my life a new and reassuring perspective.

Fear of Recovery — or, Will I Disappear Without My Defects?

A fear that surfaced secretly, one that was very hard for me to understand, was my fear of being transformed through sobriety into a person I wouldn't like. I had grown attached to myself over the years, had grown comfortable with a lot of the traits that I thought I would have to give up to stay sober. I worked long and hard on my persona — the tortured artist, the angst-ridden woman — and I didn't want to turn suddenly into a sunny, skip-down-the-road-of-life type. I was afraid of losing a lot of what I valued in myself: my sensitivity and empathy, my ability to write, my sense of the world's complexity.

I think identity is a particularly complicated issue for people in recovery. We didn't know who we were when we were drinking except that we seemed to be a mass of contradictory selves. We each struggled mightily to define an "I" amidst the whirlwind. As we remain sober, we may feel buffeted about by contradictory shoulds, and we may have trouble figuring out which voice, which self, is the "real me." Meanwhile, we often cling to the things that seem to define and make us special; we balk at the prospect of losing ourselves by surrendering to a Higher Power, to other people, to recovery.

In the Big Book, we learn that we are not always ready to give up our character defects. A big reason for this is that many of us know little of ourselves *but* our defects. Those of us who spent so many years with our disease running roughshod in our lives may not know which parts of ourselves are sick or well. For all the pain that we're feeling, we still don't want to completely let go because we have no idea what would be left.

By keeping sober, by listening to other recovering men and women, and by my willingness to try other ways of thinking about myself, I learned that many of my fears were caused by an *either/or* way of thinking. I learned that I wasn't all sick or all well. I learned that I wasn't, and would never be, all one thing or another. I was, and am, a flow, a mixture, and I can let go of some things while taking on others.

My fear of becoming a chirpy recovered robot was based on the *either/or* model. I discovered, however, that I wasn't either sensitive or insensitive, either a poet or a pedant, either a seer or a simpleton. In recovery, I found I could still empathize with pain in others — I just didn't have to take it all on myself. I didn't start writing again for a long time, but only because I'd lost a voice and subject — my endless identity crisis.

The world did not suddenly become a simple place to live in once I was sober. It was less hostile and foreboding, but it was still complex and mysterious. In many ways, the-way-I-looked-at-things-when-I-was-drinking view was more simple; there was a sameness, a predictability to how I saw my life while I was drinking. Now, I bring a sense of openness and flexibility to how I take in the world around me. I realize that my fears of giving up some of my personal qualities were groundless.

My fear of being simpleminded, of being able to speak only in clichés, turned out to be a misunderstanding of the nature of truth. Many clichés become clichés because they are so undeniably right, functioning effectively over and over again in a multiplicity of situations. And I realized that the seemingly mindless cheer that so many recovering people have in their lives is really a genuine peace of mind, a serenity, arrived at through acceptance, not ignorance.

My fears of becoming someone different, of losing my self, evaporated as I realized that I was becoming *more* myself, that what I valued most about myself was becoming more accessible and reliable, and less choked and deformed by my fears.

CHAPTER NINE

Grief

As we sober up, we feel more vulnerable because our feelings seem closer to the surface. As the wounds we inflicted on ourselves heal, we find we have a tremendous capacity for deep, intense emotional experience. We begin to remember the past more fully, and we recognize, perhaps for the first time, how much is lost forever.

Grief Helps Me Live Fully

I see the capacity to grieve as a gift of recovery. When I was drinking, and even in my early days of sobriety, I felt scared, hurt, and lonely. I cried buckets of tears, and felt very sorry for myself. That wasn't grief; it was self-pity.

Grief is a response to loss. And with every deep loss in the present, we connect again with our losses in the past. Grief is a healing process because it helps us deeply mourn and finally accept the losses we have suffered in our lives.

Mourning involves dwelling in a deep, powerful sorrow. Grief wells up in us, and we learn to sit with it awhile, to keep it company. Many older cultures have customs and rituals of mourning; in contemporary America, we have very few. Grief frightens us; we try to shoo it away by bucking up, by not crying over spilt milk, by letting bygones be bygones and getting on with life.

Yet we have suffered terrible losses. I believe we need to mourn those losses if we are to fully heal. When we sober up, we realize we may have lost our youth, our dreams, our children, our lover, our family, our friends. They, or that part of them blotted out by our drinking, cannot be returned to us. When we were drinking, we never fully grieved for these losses because we couldn't. We didn't know how.

Now that we're sober, whether we are twenty or sixty years old, we begin to see how much we have lost.

Grieving the Loss of Childhood

Many of us missed our childhoods — we became adult too soon. We rushed off or were forced into a life that had no room for laughter and play, or for dates, proms, first loves, adolescent dreams.

Grieving the Loss of Parents

Many of us lost our parents — they drank, or were abusive, or they left us either by getting sick, or divorced, or they disappeared or died. We who have lost our parents can never know what it would have been like to have them with us, giving us their love, their attention, their wisdom and support. We need to mourn our loss.

Grieving the Loss of Dreams

Our lives are in motion and we have made irrevocable decisions and commitments — the past is past. But what of the possibilities of our lost youth, our abandoned desires to be a scientist, singer, actor or actress, poet, architect, or world traveler? There is something painful and poignant about having lost the freedom to choose our lives. Our lives seemed to have happened to us without our knowing it, and we need to mourn the loss of our dreams and what might have been.

Grieving the Loss of Relationships

Those of us who raised children while we were drunk need to grieve the loss of relationships that never had a chance to develop, of the moments in our childrens' lives that can never be recaptured or relived. As important as amends are to our recovery, they cannot restore what never was — those losses must be mourned.

We have lost friends, lovers, or spouses while drinking, and we need to grieve for the loss of what those relationships could have been. We had dreams of intimacy and connection, we had glimpsed and believed in a shared future. With each loss, we lost a possible self.

Mourning allows healing. The tears we shed as we grieve are healing tears. They are a way of honoring, and of making connections to, our deepest selves. Grief allows us to fully accept the past, to finally heal the deep private wounds that all losses inflict.

As we grow in recovery, our capacity to mourn develops. Each of us can grow in our capacity for intense, abiding sadness. Sometimes a current, seemingly insignificant loss will trigger it. Sometimes a trauma — a death, an illness, a divorce — will open the door to what feels like an ocean of endless sadness. But the sorrow is not endless, nor will it swallow us up.

I'm beginning to understand my life as a tapestry of pain and pleasure, loss and gain, sadness and happiness, hardship and love. There are no guarantees, and no magic to ward off tragedy, cruelty, and pain. To live fully is to be there for *all* that comes to us, instead of trying to cover it up, rise above it, put it behind us too quickly or hide it away.

I believe that we must honor our grief, give it room in our life, and keep it company. Grieving is a deep, mysterious human process that deserves our respect. By grieving, we can better accept and transcend the tragedies of human experience. By grieving for our losses in the past, we are free to live more deeply, richly, and fully in the present.

PART III

MAKING CONNECTIONS

Addiction isolates us from our true selves, other people, and our Higher Power. Our sense of who we are is distorted, and our interactions with others often leave us feeling mentally and spiritually unhappy. For full recovery, we need access to our authentic self, so we can connect with the support of others.

CHAPTER TEN

Needing Others

We become trapped by our drinking; we spin our wheels in a no-win world that we make up. Even as I began to see that I was trapped, that maybe I could define myself and other people differently, I couldn't follow through. I couldn't change as long as I was drinking because I couldn't quit drinking long enough to change. And being dry was a worse hell than being drunk, until I was given respite from the destructive beliefs I'd learned.

I've had to learn the hard way that recovery from addiction is a shared journey. I tried to do it on my own, but made little progress as long as I cut myself off from the love and support of other recovering people. Their support gives me the freedom to explore and expand, to discover and connect.

All that I read in books, learn in counseling, or figure out on my own does me no good unless I apply it in my relationships with other people. Self-knowledge divorced from action is useless, and action divorced from self-knowledge (another way to define denial, I suspect) was what my addiction was all about.

Afraid to Be Loved,
Afraid of Not Being Loved

Odd as it may seem, there have been times in recovery when I was afraid of getting so well that I wouldn't need anyone. I was afraid of turning into someone else, of becoming a kind of super-together automaton. That person, I believed, would be domineering, insensitive, and unlovable.

I had constructed another *either/or* situation. Either I was weak and helpless, or I was strong and autonomous. I told myself if I was weak, maybe somebody would love me and take care of me. If I was strong, I wouldn't need people and they wouldn't need me. I had confused *need* with *love,* putting me in another no-win situation. I was afraid to be weak, afraid to be strong, afraid to be loved, afraid of not being loved.

These fears kept me from opening myself up to the bonds of affection that people can develop when they really share themselves. I think my fears ruled me because I felt so needy. Sometimes I felt like a gaping black hole of need that would, if I gave in to its pull, swallow anyone who came near.

So, I did the opposite. I refused affection, help, or any offer of tenderness. I defined myself as a loner, a hard-drinking, hard-living woman of the world, independent and indestructible. And at 3:00 a.m., or when the liquor hit me wrong, I would dissolve into what I feared and disdained: the needy little girl who desperately craved the tenderness, help, and affection I kept turning away.

This *either/or* division has stayed with me a long time. I can even use AA, or therapeutic jargon, to cut myself off from other people. I'll talk a good game, be "open" and "honest," and even admit that I'm hurting a little. But this act is a far cry from the kind of spontaneous trust I know is possible when I recognize and accept the genuine need I have for other people's affection and respect. I was helped tremendously when I realized that other people have this same need.

Many recovering alcoholics are wounded deeply in ways that are secret and painful. That we need others doesn't mean we are greedy or insatiable. We are healed as the needy children within us are nurtured and healed.

I think by recognizing and accepting our neediness we find ways to connect with our deepest, most private selves. When we find ways to love and care for ourselves, we have more of that to share with other people. That terrible hunger, once so powerful that it frightened us, fades. We find ourselves giving and receiving affection, respect, attention, and love. It feels wonderful.

How I Learned to Trust

Our capacity for good feelings seems to be based in our capacity for trust. I learned in recovery groups that it is possible to trust. When you are surrounded by people who care for that vulnerable child within you, you can heal. When they consistently support and nurture your tentative, feeble attempts to grow, you can learn to trust.

In a supportive environment, where others are taking the same risks, we can gently develop faith in the essential goodness of others. To be open and honest is risky. We feel vulnerable. But with each attempt that is met with understanding and acceptance, trust develops. In an atmosphere of support, I realized that my fears of being known, revealed, or exposed are not necessary, that being weak is part of being human, that needing other people is natural. Trusting in and caring for others is scary sometimes, and it hurts sometimes, but is mostly a relief.

I'm learning to take appropriate emotional risks, but I still have a lot of learning to do. I'm not very good at opening up gradually, or choosing who to trust. In early recovery I went from being a loner to being a heat-seeking device: indiscriminate warmth in search of reciprocal warmth. I felt, sometimes, like a pendulum that always shoots past the mark: I saw where I wanted to be just as I sailed past it, off to the other extreme. I don't recommend this mode of learning, but, for me, it *was* progress. At least I glimpsed the middle ground as I sailed by!

What I learned, while swinging wildly between trust and mistrust, fear and fearlessness, is that the world doesn't come to an end if I open up, and then get hurt or rejected. I'll still pick wrong at times; I'll trust people who turn on me, lie to me, who don't deserve the faith I place in them. And this will always be painful. There's no way around the fact that it hurts when someone betrays my trust.

And, of course, I'll still want to beat myself up for being so blind, so stupid . . . until I remember that I don't have to anymore. What I've realized is that with recovery comes resilience. Recovery gives me the emotional, mental, and spiritual tools to pick myself up, dust myself off, and try again.

Tired of Playing the Princess

I felt fragile when I was drinking, and maybe I was. When people didn't come through for me and let me down, when I screwed up, whenever things went awry, I took it to heart. I saw it as more evidence of my essential unworthiness, their essential cruelty, the hopelessness of having a decent relationship with anybody. I didn't think I could trust myself, so I couldn't trust others.

As an alcoholic, I have been my own worst enemy, a far harsher critic of myself than anyone else. What I was afraid of and mistrusted the most was myself-in-other-people: the tyrant voice that would judge me and find me wanting. When I found out that most other people are just as afraid as I am, and when I found out that responding to them with acceptance usually means that they accept me, the world became a kinder, safer place.

Recovery is turning out to be very different from what I feared "being well" would be. I used to believe that being well meant being totally together. With my *either/or* way of looking at things, I thought that if the "drinking me" was sick and weak and needy and helpless, the "well me" would be healthy and strong and never need anyone. The "well me" was an image I concocted when I was drinking. It was a combination of advertising (sleek woman striding down the street, dressed for success, on her own and loving it), self-help books (looking out for number one, being assertive, totally organized, a one-minute manager), and my tyrant voice (don't feel, be productive, be perfect).

My goal, it seemed, was to become a human dynamo, invulnerable, without flaws, without weakness, inhuman. But anything that looked like it might make me less vulnerable or less flawed was scary, since I really didn't want to turn into a human dynamo. It sounded mighty lonely.

And I was lonely when I tried it. Being totally together takes a tremendous amount of energy, and, in fact, is a myth. The facade always cracks. I know that my hem has a safety pin in it, that my closets are crammed with crud. I get tired of being Princess Grace to everybody, no matter how they treat me. My shiny floors and spotless dishes didn't make me feel any better about myself. The promised glamour of a high-powered career provided pretty low wattage on the inside. Now, every time I try to live like the "total woman," I feel like I've been sold a bill of goods. I have been. We all have.

Recovery has not turned me into a flawless person, and that's a real relief. It has given me the chance to be human, not a robot. I manage (most of the time) to get work done, meet people, have friends, do laundry, buy groceries, pay the bills, and generally enjoy a pretty fine life — not perfectly, not consistently, not always right on time, and not without some grumbling and screwups, but pretty well. And *all* of it, even the worst minute, is better than when I was drinking.

CHAPTER ELEVEN

Caretaking and Isolation

Alcoholism has been called a disease of isolation, and it's no wonder — as drunks we had such a lousy time with other people. Not only did we learn how to hide the ravages of our disease from others, but we also learned that our addictive ways of being with others causes all kinds of misery. Maybe one of the reasons some of us continue to become isolated in sobriety is because our attempts at relationships before recovery caused us so much pain and confusion.

Becoming "Undependent"

During my drinking days, I alternated between being aloof and alone and throwing myself into dramatic, intense, destructive relationships. Either I was painfully, proudly separate, or I was enmeshed in an emotional whirlwind. Much of my desire to isolate myself was due to the outcome of my relationships: I'd get hurt, then retreat to lick my wounds, vowing never to repeat my mistakes. But a few months later, I'd fling myself out to get hurt again.

Sobriety did not magically change this pattern, but what I eventually learned in recovery helped me see that something was terribly wrong with the way I had gone about being with others. I was in recovery several years before I was willing, or even able, to directly confront this crucial aspect of healing. I'd heard about *enabling* and *codependency*, and I'd even tried a few Al-Anon meetings. But I wasn't willing, and perhaps just not ready, early on, to address the underlying causes of my twisted connections to other people.

Codependency explains the predictable pattern my relationships took on. Drunk or sober, I rushed to rescue others (or hoped they would rescue me), then got angry and resentful when they wouldn't get saved (or wouldn't save me). Even in recovery, I spent endless hours trying to figure out what was going wrong, why my friendships were uncomfortable, my love life a disaster, my work life a series of tensions and anxieties. I was sober, wasn't I? Wasn't I living One Day at a Time, trying to practice recovery principles in all my affairs? I thought if other people would just act right, everything would be much better. I would ruefully claim that "if it weren't for other people, I'd be just fine."

Without the love and care of other people, recovery from alcoholism would be a lonely triumph. Yes, we'd be free from the pains of drunkenness, hangovers, lost weekends, and crazy thoughts, but we would have little in our lives beyond freedom from the ravages of alcohol. I believe that recovery is more than freedom *from* alcohol: it is also freedom *to* risk, love, learn, change, and grow. Recovery from addiction opens up a new world full of people to share our new lives with.

In order to share this world of continuing recovery, I needed to learn a new way of being with others. The key for me was understanding how codependency had defined so many of my relationships, and then becoming willing to change that, little by little. I am now learning, constantly, what it means to become "undependent."

Opening Another Can of Worms

Recovering women seem to struggle with codependency more than men. The longer we are in recovery, the more obvious it becomes that, even though we know a lot about our own defects and are working our program to the best of our abilities, we still can, and do

- fall in love with people who seem to need us to take care of them, or who need to dominate us.

- rush into Twelve Stepping and giving advice, eagerly seeking to "help" others recover.
- form intense, demanding friendships, and then we get hurt and angry when our friends let us down or take advantage of us.
- take on more and more responsibilities at home and at work, agonizing over problems we can't solve.
- seek to soothe, smooth out, or control each and every situation in which we find ourselves.

The inevitable result is that we become exhausted, frustrated, resentful, and full of rage that all our best efforts to make things "right" meet with little success. All along, we know somehow that our recovery is at risk, that all we cherish about our newfound emotional honesty, hard-won serenity, and fragile self-esteem is challenged by what happens to us when we are involved with the "real world."

Ironically, understanding ourselves as alcoholics does not automatically help us understand our frustrating pattern of relationships. To understand that, we need to turn to the insights of those who have struggled to live with us. Many of us have found, to our surprise, that Al-Anon offers tremendous support and guidance in helping us learn how to create and maintain healthy relationships. Adult Children of Alcoholics, other support groups, and reading self-help literature on dysfunctional families may also be helpful.

This is a bitter pill to swallow. Isn't it enough to cope with our chemical dependency? Must we now also open up this new can of worms? Having worked so hard to recognize and change our addictive characteristics, must we now figure out and deal with some new syndrome called codependency?

For many of us, I'm afraid the answer is yes. Almost everything we learned about relationships while we were growing up, or while we were practicing addicts, has to be revised. We learned about relationships from our families, which were often dysfunctional, and our loved ones, who were often addicts too. What we know about ourselves-with-others is soaked in the deforming swamp of addiction. We need to learn new ways of believing, thinking, and acting if we are to find ways to form healthy, healing relationships.

Once again, there are no magic rules or easy plans, with absolute guarantees. Once again, we have to come to the painful awareness of our own powerlessness; then we have to surrender, "clean house," and seek a Power greater than ourselves. And once again, we will long for easier, softer ways. We will rebel and complain; we will become close-minded and resentful, and we will deny we are codependent until we are finally brought to our knees. At least that's what it's been like for me.

Discovering the Patterns in My Relationships

Caretaking can masquerade itself as support, concern, warmth, and caring. Women are especially vulnerable to becoming codependent because we are "supposed to be" the caretakers: selfless, nurturing wives, lovers, mothers, and friends. As a woman, I was told I was better at emotional sustenance, at intuitively understanding others' needs and ministering to them so that I should be able to offer anyone and everyone support and guidance.

Not only is this ideal unattainable, but it is also sexist and unfair. It is based on the assumption that women are mysteriously gifted, and that we owe others something we ourselves don't or shouldn't need.

Caring, nurturing, accepting, and forgiving are wonderful human qualities. The problems come when we

- offer these qualities because it's what we feel we *ought* to do.
- deny ourselves these qualities while offering them to others.
- pretend we feel these good qualities when, instead, we are full of hostility and resentment.
- give these qualities to make ourselves feel superior to those we supposedly "help."

I've found plenty of people in my life who seemed willing to let me help them. In trying to help them, I've felt virtuous and powerful. In the midst of my worst alcoholic drinking, I still chronically offered advice, sympathy, time, and attention to those I deemed more needy than me.

The only way I seemed to be able to have friends was to find out what was hurting them, and then get them to talk about it. If they weren't open, I'd decode them; I'd try to figure out what they really felt, and then I'd share my insights with them. The only way I knew to work with others was to "fix" the situation — figure out what was really wrong, and then try to set things right. I was like a maniacal Florence Nightingale, flying to the side of whatever wounded person, place, or thing I could find.

The resulting exhaustion, resentment, and anguish were excruciating, especially once I was sober. I recognized that a few of my friends were professional victims — people who seemed to delight in their misfortunes. While I was seeking to work through my pain, they seemed to be wallowing in theirs. I resented what I perceived as their attempts to drag me down with them. I also recognized, among my friends, some growing resentments toward me. I noticed some sniping, criticism, and even hostility at my self-righteousness and my relentless efforts to tell them what to do.

I also discovered a pattern in my relationships with men. I sought "diamonds in the rough" to polish and make shine . . . only to have them stubbornly remain lumps of coal. Even my new marriage was slowly being strangled by my attempts to "fix my husband," to turn him into a victim who needed my wisdom and insight to become whole.

I felt tangled up in unhealthy, unsatisfying relationships. To make it simple, and to keep myself on top, I tried to blame everybody else. I tried to tell myself that I just seemed to pick victims and losers, that all I needed was to find some healthy new friends and I'd be just fine. My old companions — denial, sitting in judgment, and false pride — were back again. I had many wonderful people in my life, but I never knew how to appreciate their true qualities. I thought that for me to be a good person (read: caretaker), they had to be victims, to need me. The problem was mostly in me, and in my incessant attempts to cure what I thought ailed them.

CHAPTER TWELVE

Finding Ourselves

I came to a point where I had to confront this compulsion to control others with kindness. While on the surface I tried to maintain a serene, calm (read: superior) demeanor, inside I was a seething mass of hostility. How *dare* these people be so dependent on me, so parasitic, so helpless and weak? How *dare* they get angry and hostile, even try to reject me, after all I've done for them? How *dare* they not get well? I felt like I was going crazy.

Detachment Doesn't Mean Turning to Ice

A healthy alternative to this, I learned, is detachment. How cruel and cold that sounded! It meant putting *my* needs first. I thought I would be disliked, criticized, and attacked, that I would become a bad person. What would happen to all those people if I stopped trying to save them?

And what *were* my own needs, anyway? I had spent so long deciphering other people's supposed needs that I wasn't very good at recognizing my own. Inside me was a raging little girl, who by now was clenching her fists, stamping her feet, and screaming, "Pay attention to me . . . take me seriously . . . LISTEN TO ME!"

"Hah!" the tyrant in my head responded. "Screaming will get you nowhere, young lady. If you ask nicely, then maybe I'll think about it."

No wonder I felt like I was going nuts. I wanted too much to be "well." I wanted to be a good friend, a loving wife, a caring teacher, to be loved and admired, and most of all, to get everybody else (especially that little girl in me) to straighten up and act right. All my efforts to be all those things seemed to be unraveling. I alternated between trying my old ways even harder and trying what I thought was detachment, which to me meant turning into an unfeeling block of ice.

I struggled between the extremes of intense emotional commitment and cold, unemotional rejection. By listening to the people in Al-Anon and Adult Children of Alcoholics, I began to see that these are not the only choices available. Once again, my rigid *either/or* thinking had backed me into an impossible corner.

There *is* another option, one that allows the love, compassion, and nurturing that I value — without the hostility, resentment, and frustration. When I began to see that detachment means disconnecting from the enmeshment of caretaking and control, and not disconnecting from other people, I began to recover.

Before I could fully understand detachment, I had to see how many of my relationships were based on an addictive pattern, on a "what's in it for me" attitude with me trying to make other people give me what I wanted. Facing this allowed me to recognize the many meaningful connections that are possible with others, and to finally discover the healing and growth possible in respectful and honest relationships.

Boundaries Are Lines of Love

Boundaries are not walls, but markers. They mark where I am and where you are. They help us be responsible for, and beholden to, ourselves. They tell us that we are separate, equal human beings, finding each other in a world of possibilities.

My boundaries got blurred by caretaking because I tried to take responsibility for others' pain, unhappiness, discomfort, and addictions. I saw sharing burdens as the way to show care for others. Now, I'm learning a different way of caring: to observe, accept, and comfort, but not to take on what belongs to another person.

By recognizing and maintaining my boundaries, I recognize what is mine and what is someone else's. I realize that I can be of most service by maintaining that distinction. Each of us finds our own way, certainly by the example and support of others, but eventually by being true to our inner self and our Higher Power. All the elaborate, well-meaning, codependent involvement I know so well and have practiced so long has never done any good. People change when they want to, not when I want them to. They become who they choose to become, not who I want them to be.

Boundaries are lines of love. They not only define an inside, but also an outside line, where we can meet with others fully and freely. When boundaries get blurred, relationships develop hooks and claws, hidden defenses, and mixed signals. When boundaries are clear, we meet each other wholeheartedly, giving and receiving what each of us freely offers.

If we maintain boundaries, our identities are not at stake in our relationships, nor do we become defined by another's need of us. We do not rely on others' evaluations of us to tell us who we are. We become able to clearly see our own strengths and weaknesses, to see where we end and another begins.

Discovering My Values and Beliefs

We cannot recognize where we end and another person begins unless we clearly and consistently recognize who we are and where we stand. For me, this means learning what my values and purposes are and being able to define myself and act on my own beliefs. It means acknowledging the child within me as a source of spontaneity, dreams, and wonder.

I believe that the child within each of us can help us learn who we are and what we want, if we listen. What that child has to say may often seem unrealistic and unworkable, but to that child the impulses are authentic. Our child can tell us what is special about us, what is right for us, and what is uniquely ours. Defining our values and learning about ourselves is a process of recognizing and accepting ourselves as unique people with a core of beliefs that we know and act from.

I have much in common with others, and there is always much to learn from whoever I meet. But I am not "just like" someone else, and my attempts to be "just like" another person are attempts to people-please, to gain the acceptance and approval of those around me at the expense of myself. My attempts to be "just like" some ideal self — benevolent, caring, and wise are equally destructive. When I do this, I am listening to the tyrant in my head, not my heart; I am listening to my shoulds, not my inner child.

In my drinking days, I longed desperately to fit in. Meanwhile, I proudly and stubbornly clung to the qualities that I felt made me different. In my early recovery, I was so frightened of self-will, and of the cunning power of alcoholism that I mistrusted my own perceptions and desires. I often blindly followed and repeated the advice and suggestions of others.

I could sound like a "good AA," but I was not speaking from my heart. In fact, I knew very little of what was in my heart. I was hardly able to listen to my own small, uncertain voice. I have gone through painful periods of estrangement, times when I feel disconnected from the program, other recovering people, the outside world, myself, and my Higher Power. I now see these periods (as with all painful times in recovery) as tremendously valuable for learning about myself.

Staying Centered — Maintaining a Healthy Balance

For me, staying centered requires cultivating an essential, private core of beliefs and values that are genuinely, deeply my own. If I feel, think, act, and speak from this core, I can be at peace with myself and with others. Then, I am aware of my boundaries. I feel free to take pleasure in others, and I feel mentally, emotionally, and spiritually healthy. When I don't act, think, or speak from this core, I lose track of my center by trying to please others, by placing unrealistic expectations on myself and them, or by believing that I have the responsibility and the power to fix things. When that happens, my energy turns into anxiety.

Caretaking is not some single issue that can be separated from everything else, examined, and then "taken care of." It can pervade all aspects of who we are, and how we live and act in the world. Learning how to establish and maintain rewarding relationships means learning new ways of being in the world. We need, as always, to be patient, loving, and kind to ourselves as we learn how to connect without controlling, how to love without manipulating, and how to give freely and fully of ourselves to others.

Each of us has special gifts and purposes; these continue to be revealed to us in sobriety as we learn who we are in relation to others. The paradox is that we can't be at ease with others unless we are at ease with ourselves, and we can't be at ease with ourselves unless we know what is right for us — apart from other people. In the following chapters, I'll explore that part of my journey where I discovered how this knowledge is affirmed and supported by my spiritual program. Through quiet times of meditation and prayer, what I call *trusting contemplation*, I become aware of what is right for me, where my center is, and I begin to have the faith to act accordingly. Through faith, I find the courage to change.

PART IV

BECOMING WHOLE

The world of the addict is fragmented. We learned to live as multiple selves, with different faces to present to what we saw as a hostile, judgmental world. We heard and tried to follow different voices that told us contradictory things about who and how we must be. We made desperate, aimless attempts to connect these fragments, to create a coherent, integrated self. In recovery, we find ways to reconnect, to restore a wholeness to our shattered world.

CHAPTER THIRTEEN

Cultivating Faith

Addiction blocks us from a Higher Power by trapping us in an endless cycle of self-will. Recovery breaks that cycle. Recovery from addiction is spiritual as well as physical, mental, and emotional. A rich new relationship with a Power greater than ourselves becomes possible. Spiritual faith does not necessarily swoop down on us in a blinding flash, but may instead be developed and cultivated by committed and consistent spiritual practice.

Sunlight of the Spirit

Spirituality may be the most personal aspect of recovery. A relationship with a Higher Power is intensely private, and each of us finds our own ways to develop and maintain faith.

In my early recovery, when the whole concept of a spiritual program seemed alien and strange, I listened closely to those around me, trying to discover what their secret was. The only common denominator I found was that other recovering people trusted in some kind of Power that was greater than themselves. Beyond that, there were many differences. I was told by other recovering people that each of us cultivates, and gains sustenance from, our own spiritual path.

In the quiet of our own hearts and minds, as well as in the fellowship of others, we can hear the stirrings of our own spirituality. For me, it is through grace that I become open, willing, and honest enough to recover from this destructive disease of addiction. Grace gives me access to a healing power. I think of my Higher Power as a healing power, and I use the Big Book phrase the "sunlight of the spirit" to name that healing power.

My faith, then, is that there is a healing force available to us with qualities best described by the phrase, the "sunlight of the spirit." This healing force is always there if I am willing to seek it and let it into my life. It can sustain me through times of doubt and confusion. It can guide me in making decisions and choices and comfort me in times of sorrow and despair.

Blocking the Sunlight

Active alcoholism all but completely blocked me from the sunlight of the spirit. Even in sobriety, after years of dry time, I can still block myself from healing by putting up all kinds of barriers and resistance. This is, I believe, my disease reasserting itself in all its cunning, baffling power. But this may also be simply a part of the human condition — one of the ways we all, at times, tend to cut ourselves off from the possibilities of life.

Our reprieve from alcoholism is, as the Big Book says, a daily reprieve, contingent on the maintenance of a fit spiritual condition. For me, maintenance work is quiet time, time when I seek to silence the hubbub of my self-will and let in the healing power that I believe is there for me and for all of us.

Maintaining my awareness of a healing power throughout the day can ground and center me. The days when I carry with me the vision of sunlight are my best days. Then, I am calm, serene, and at ease with myself and others. But such a vision is always at risk because I can easily slip back into my old ways of feeling, thinking, and acting.

There are five ways that I am still most likely to block this sense of a Power greater than myself in my life, ways that seem to be common for many other recovering people struggling for spiritual meaning. They are *dishonesty, perfectionism, self-will, depression,* and *fear*.

Dishonesty

It is still too easy for me to lie to myself and others, especially about how well I am. I think my false pride, along with some residual caretaking tendencies, makes me want to appear wise, together, and fully recovered. I am still unwilling to admit that I sometimes have petty, crummy thoughts, and I am reluctant to let others see that I am flawed, imperfect — human.

Emotional dishonesty blocks me from other people. But it also blocks me from my fullest self and from my healing Higher Power.

It is my healing Higher Power I call on to help me become willing to be honest with myself and others, to accept myself and all my flaws, and to share my struggles instead of trying to hide them away. Once *willing*, I become *able* to be honest with myself and others. When I recover honestly, I become available to the love and support that was always there.

Perfectionism

The addict in me can easily imagine a world full of people, and even a Higher Power, who are constantly evaluating me. I assume that they want me to be perfect. I also assume that I'm so important and so imperfect that they will tote up a list of my failures and flaws, then banish me forever.

That part of me can still believe that there is a single, narrow path of recovery, and that I'm not doing it "right." This is another aspect of perfectionism: my alcoholic belief in a black-and-white world of right and wrong, good and bad, and of secret rules I haven't yet discovered. Whether I apply these beliefs to myself, to others, or to my recovery, I'm left in a cold and lonely place.

My faith in the sunlight of the spirit, whose healing power is all-encompassing, allows me to escape the prison of perfectionism. When I imagine a *meadow* of recovery instead of a path, an *open field* instead of a straight and narrow way, a *sun-drenched arena* instead of a spot-lit stage, I become aware of how confining and unhappy my perfectionist thinking is. Who am I to judge myself or others? Who am I to think I know what is perfect, or even what is best, everytime?

When I lighten up a little, relax, and am grateful, I become open to the goodness around me — the manifestations of love, the infinite delights of grace. My faith reminds me that in the sunlight of the spirit, there is not one single, final, distant, perfect reward, but an infinite number of pleasures and possibilities nearby.

Self-Will

I can still easily put myself at the center of the universe and believe that somehow I can control people, places, and things, and that I have the big responsibility of keeping things going.

Self-will leads me to

- take on all kinds of duties and tasks that aren't mine.
- become frustrated and enraged when things don't go my way.
- rush into projects and plans.
- demand certain kinds of outcomes.
- tug whatever strings I can grab hold of to make things go my way.
- become a whirlwind of activity, but empty at the center of my being.

By filling my world with my will, I leave no room for spiritual replenishment. I become exhausted and empty, surrounded only by my frustration. In time, I recognize again that my self-will is causing my pain. Self-will always prevents me from being quiet, aware, and open to what is all around me because I am too full of myself to let anything else in.

True humility, I believe, lies in recognizing that we are part of a vast, mysterious, ongoing universe. We can flow with it or we can fight against it every step of the way. Self-will is fighting; it is going against the grain. False pride is assuming that we somehow have the power to understand and alter the universe by our own actions. Both are based on a lack of trust in the flow, on what will happen if we Let Go and Let God.

Trusting the flow of the universe, and trusting in the natural, inevitable healing power of the spirit, requires humility. It means letting go of the belief that I can *control* the universe, and leaving room for the faith that I can *contribute* to it. I am part of, but not central to, the universe. And when I remember that distinction, I can let go of my desperate, driven actions and let in faith. I can think, feel, and act in concert with others, not as if I'm in control of them. I can act in harmonious, not discordant ways. And in that harmony, I can find the joy of genuine fulfillment.

Depression

There are times, however, when joy seems an ancient memory. In my sobriety, there have been long gray days of depression that settled down on me like a chronic, low grade fever. Then, I do not feel anxious or full of self-will. I sometimes cannot locate the character defect, person, place, or thing that is making me feel so low. I just feel empty and sad. It is as if my sunlight has gone behind a cloud for no particular reason. I go about my daily business, but I feel listless and aimless. What once seemed appealing and pleasant now seems useless and uninteresting. A pervasive gloom settles around me, coloring everything in shades of gray and brown.

I do not know what causes these episodes of depression, but I do know how to limit their effects. When I simply remain open to the *possibility* of a healing power that is greater than myself, I am able to live quietly through these times and accept that, just for now, my sunlight is behind a cloud. I try to use these times for resting, for gathering the strength and energy for when my sun will come out again.

These gray days give me a chance to gently and patiently examine my life. I can examine without taking action or making decisions. These are the days that I learn to "do the next right thing" without questioning. These are the days when I truly trudge the road of recovery. These are also, I believe, the days when I am growing and changing in invisible ways, when my feelings of emptiness and uselessness are masking the deep healing that I must, for now, take on faith. During my gray days, my faith in the possibility of healing is taken to another level.

Of course, I can more easily believe in a loving, healing Higher Power when I am full of energy and light than when light and energy seem to have left my life forever. But if I believe in the possibility of healing, even when I can't immediately feel its power, then always, eventually, little shafts of pleasure, tiny beams of energy, and brief moments of joy reenter my life. If I remain open to the possibility that light and joy will reenter my life, they always return. That is, for me, one of the surprising gifts of my recovery —the ability, in hours of darkness, to believe that the sun will shine again.

Fear

Among the most precious gifts of recovery is the possibility of change. As we live sober lives, we are offered all kinds of opportunities — for new relationships, new jobs, new places, new paths. We often seek these as we clear away the wreckage of our past and discover what has been denied and hidden from us in our alcoholism. With our newfound tools of recovery as talismans, we eagerly embrace these opportunities. But sometimes in the midst of our plans for change, we find ourselves terrified.

Fear seems to swoop down suddenly, paralyzing us. I have seen many succumb to an intense, devastating fear, just as we are on the verge of a life-changing recognition, decision, or plan. It is as if we suddenly lose all faith in our recovery and our Higher Power at the very moment when we are about to take actions that our faith makes possible.

I think of this paralyzing fear as our disease's last-ditch effort to keep us trapped. If active alcoholism traps us in a downward spiral, and recovery offers us a way into an open field of possibility, then fear is the way our disease keeps us standing still in that field, too frightened to move.

Sometimes the fear is so paralyzing that we can't even pray. We are wracked by doubt and feel as if we've been abandoned by everyone and everything. This fear can feel more like a physical pain than emotional discomfort, and it can be so relentless that we want an escape of any kind. We yearn for the contentment and peace of mind that was ours only recently. We try everything we have learned so far in recovery to recapture that serenity, but whatever tools worked before now seem to mock us. The wise words of the program, our friends, and our favorite spiritual literature seem hollow, pointless, and empty. This pain is especially hard to bear if we have had months or years of contented sobriety. It is as if the slate has been suddenly wiped clean, and we are back where we started — alone, frightened, helpless, and hopeless.

Maybe we are, in some ways, back where we started. The Twelve Steps provide an ongoing process of renewing our faith and our commitment to recovery. When we embrace the Steps for the first time, our primary goal is to escape the pain of active addiction. They offer us a way to overcome our disease, One Day at a Time. But again and again in our recovery, we are given opportunities to overcome our disease, manifested not only as active addiction, but also as the helplessness and hopelessness that are its hallmarks. These manifestations of addiction often seem to appear when we are preparing ourselves for a new, unfamiliar phase of recovery.

The fear that sometimes accompanies major life changes can be used as an opportunity to renew our program, to rediscover open-mindedness, honesty, and the willingness to begin again. It allows us to surrender again, to again admit our powerlessness, to again believe that we can be restored to sanity, and to return our will and our lives over to the care of a Power greater than ourselves.

When we use this dread as an opportunity to renew our program, we often find a richer, more joyous, and more faith-filled recovery on the other side of it. By enduring, we may discover new capacities for surrender and acceptance, and paradoxically, renewed faith in a caring God.

The Big Book tells us that God's will for us is to be happy, joyous, and free. It does not say that such a state is automatic or constant. I believe that true faith in recovery is faith in the *possibility* of happiness, joy, and freedom for us all. Faith in such a possibility allows us to courageously live through the testing times, the periods where all good things seem to have disappeared.

Believing deeply, with humility and commitment, that we each deserve a rich, rewarding recovery, and that it is indeed God's will for us, can help guide and comfort us through the dark times.

CHAPTER FOURTEEN

Unity and Clarity

Our recovery gives us the opportunity to restore unity and clarity in our lives as we begin reconnecting the seemingly disparate selves created by our addiction. Recovery must pervade every aspect of our lives if balance and harmony are to be restored.

Healing mental and emotional wounds, making connections within myself and to others, and cultivating faith in a Higher Power have made my recovery a journey from fragmentation toward wholeness. I experience wholeness to the degree that I have an ongoing sense of unity and clarity in my life.

My Voices Coalesce

The multiple selves and voices that jostled around in me, clamoring for attention and action, were often even more confusing and contradictory after I stopped drinking. I knew that I had to learn ways to acknowledge these voices without succumbing to them, to hear what they were really saying to me. I am learning to reject the voices that are harmful, such as the voice of the perfectionist or the caretaker, and I am learning how to listen to and cherish the voices that ask me to be true to myself, that remind me to practice honesty, humility, and compassion.

In my addiction, I lost an authentic sense of self, a center from where I could know my true desires. In recovery, the healing voices within me began to coalesce, to become a chorus of support for the voice of my inner child: the one voice who had never been given much of a chance.

That deep, authentic voice of the child in me, with all her energy, enthusiasm, hope, and desire, became a touchstone for my healing. I learned to rely on her to speak clearly and directly. Through her, I connect with an inner joyousness that is a precious gift of recovery.

Making Joy a Part of My Life

In my early recovery, joy was a new feeling for me. It seemed vaguely familiar, but had somehow gotten lost in the drunken shuffle of trying to control my life. And there wasn't much room for rejoicing in a life that was a constant struggle to maintain what I called "the facade of function." By keeping such a tight grip on myself, by evaluating myself against impossibly high standards, and by trying to do and be what I thought other people wanted, I created a life that was relentless and grim. My release was drinking. But it was also my captor.

I was always longing for happiness, drunk or sober. I believed that if I just worked hard enough, looked in the right places, and found a new regimen to guide me, happiness would be there at the end of the road, waiting as my reward.

Early in sobriety, I had a few weeks of what's called the "pink cloud" experience, a beautiful, hazy sense of release, excitement, and possibilities. It was so amazing to be sober, to have new friends and have hope! They warned me about the pink cloud, because they said it could leave me and I might come down from it with a thud. But it had a purpose in giving me a taste of the genuine exuberance that can become part of a sober life.

That exuberance is part of my life only to the extent that I let it be. I still sometimes revert to patterns of thought that I used while I was drinking to sabotage any possibility of joy. Yet, part of the healing of recovery has been a growing awareness of the ways I've cut myself off from my sunlight of the spirit and how I've prevented myself from being truly happy.

This awareness comes not just from not drinking, but from letting myself learn from other people. I've heard recovery compared to an onion (that is peeled layer by layer), or to a plate of spaghetti (that is untangled strand by strand). It reminds me of the La Brea tar pits in Los Angeles, where over the centuries the bones of prehistoric animals work themselves up to the surface. Each of these metaphors describes a gradual, ongoing process that reveals more and more as it continues. We realize things bit by bit, as they surface, get untangled or peeled away.

These realizations can come in a rush at first, almost too fast. Early recovery can be a tricky time, when the option of drinking has particular appeal because it seems like a quick way out of our confusing emotions. But it's also a very special time because the exuberance is so new and so intense. It's a time to stick close to other recovering people and to be open to everything they suggest. As time goes on, the exhilaration that is a gift of shared, ongoing sobriety becomes a regular part of our lives.

I regularly see a joyful connectedness in old-timers that I catch only a glimpse of in the newly sober. Recovery certainly doesn't bring total bliss; it can seem like an endless trudge at times, where there's always more to learn, more to think about, more to work on. But if we don't drink, and if we work our programs with emotional honesty and openness, the joy of connection returns because we learn to let it. Being in recovery doesn't guarantee constant joy, but it makes joy always a possibility.

The Twice-Born

As recovering alcoholics, many of us have gone through a kind of private hell and transcended it. In his book, *The Varieties of Religious Experience*, William James calls people like us the *twice-born*. The twice-born are people who have lived for a while in discordance and fragmentation. They go through a time of soul- sickness or despair, and then, through a transforming experience, find a unified self. The *once-born*, in contrast, seem to remain placid. For them, the world is pretty straightforward, a place where things usually add up and make sense.

All the recovering addicts I know are twice-born men and women. We have transcended the discordant reality we lived for so long and have become something else. We are still ourselves, but now we are integrated, whole, and renewed. It is the quality of our joy that distinguishes us, I think. This joy has much in common with the kind of joy you find in people who have recovered from other life-threatening illnesses, or who have found ways to accept and transcend personal tragedy.

For me, this capacity for joy is due to my connection to and acceptance of the healing power of the sunlight of the spirit. I envision it all around me always; as I open myself to it, my natural response is happiness. I believe it has always been there, but I was too choked with my addictive thoughts, beliefs, fears, and doubts to let it in. Even though I can and still do block myself from it, I have a sense of how much I lose when I do. I know what I'm missing now.

I first, and most reliably, began to sense that spirit in other recovering men and women. They seemed especially alive with a spiritual connection. But a healing joyousness bubbles up among all kinds of people. In the right circumstances, I've known it to flow through myself and those around me, and when that's happened, I've known instinctively that this is the way we are meant to be: happy, joyous, and free.

CHAPTER FIFTEEN

Choices and Gifts

Inner joy can become our guide as we face one of the most compelling and frightening gifts of recovery — all the new possibilities. As unity and clarity come into our life, so do new choices. We can, for possibly the first time in our life, choose how we want to live, what we want to do, where we want to be, and who we want to become. Possibilities are all around us. In recovery, we develop the ability to act on those possibilities, if we choose.

Who to be and how to be in a world where I have choices has proven to be the most exciting and frightening aspect of my recovery. Having to make choices is, I suppose, what most nonaddicted people experience and learn as they mature. But for me, that I have choices each day often seems a sudden and startling revelation.

In recovery, each of us develops the ability to recognize good and bad choices. Good choices enhance our recovery; bad choices divert us from it. Good choices free us to be ourselves; bad choices fragment us and pull us apart. To help us make choices, we can use our developing connection to our inner voice, and our trust in the wisdom of other recovering friends.

Choice is scary. It always involves a trip into the unknown. To choose to change how we react, to let go of old ways, to alter our relationships is always frightening. To choose to say good-bye to the familiar, no matter how uncomfortable it may have become, is disrupting and disorienting. The door is opened to doubt, fear, and shame — our old addictive companions.

The tools of recovery are vital to us as we prepare to act on our choices.

- Our feelings of intuition and the voice of our inner child can reassure us that we are indeed on the verge of making a healing choice.
- Our recognition that our fears are based on the catastrophic thinking of all-or-nothing beliefs can help us see our choices more realistically.
- Our developing sense of self can help us remember that we deserve good things, that the anxiety we feel about abandoning old patterns is part of our addictive thinking, not part of our recovery thinking.
- Our commitment to recovery gives us access to a support network wherever we choose to go and whatever we choose to do. There are always friends available to us, if we are willing to reach out to them.

Change is essentially a private experience, but is more likely to happen with the support of the Twelve Step program and its members. We no longer have to be alone. And finally, if the choices we make move us toward growth and away from hurting ourselves and others, we will be cultivating our connection to a Higher Power who we can rely on to heal, console, and guide us.

Using Our Gifts

I have had times when I felt guilty about receiving the tremendous gifts of recovery while others I know continue to struggle with their addiction. I wonder why I have been so blessed, so fortunate. How can I ever repay what has been so freely given to me? Obviously, I still struggle with low self-esteem. But I think there is more going on than just that. I believe that there are reasons, though they are beyond my understanding, for why some people are given the opportunity to recover. I also believe that with that opportunity comes a responsibility to fully develop my potential.

Each of us is gifted. Not only have we been given the gift of sobriety, but we have also been given the gift of developing our talents and abilities; drinking blocks us from the full expression of our gifts. Recovery gives us access to them.

In recovery, we can discover and express whatever our temperaments and talents offer. We can choose to cultivate and develop our skills, and use them in the service of what we value and believe in. We can find and do work that has meaning for us. We can contribute to the world in whatever ways we choose.

We learned, while drinking, to contain and divert our gifts. As we remain sober, we discover that we need to unlearn that pattern of containment and diversion. Whatever chokes our inner self stifles our ability to recognize and use our gifts. We remain disconnected and unfulfilled until we begin to express our potential.

As we become whole, we become a conduit for the sunlight of the spirit. That, for me, is "practicing these principles in all our affairs." I honor the gift of recovery by using my gifts.

Honorable Living

Having been given the gift of sobriety and shown how to grow and change, we can express our gratitude on a daily basis. We can do this, I believe, by living honorably. We learn how to honor ourselves, others, and our Higher Power. Honorable living is honest living on every level. It is living in clear connection with our inner voice, and in conscious contact with a Higher Power, while respecting the autonomy of others.

I can honor myself each day by listening closely to, and acting in concert with, my inner voice. I can act in ways that are self-caring, that minister to my deepest values and convictions. I can gently but firmly turn away from the destructive voices that still return, telling me to be what others want me to be. I can offer my inner child a day of joyful awareness and right action.

I can honor others by appreciating their choices and by celebrating them. I can let go of my judgments and pay attention to what is honest and whole in them. My impatience, pettiness, resentment, and frustration come from my expectations that others should act as I want them to. I can honor them by respecting their right to be and do what they choose. I can ask for the same respect, seeking out those who support me in my choices.

I can honor my Higher Power by letting the sunlight of the spirit guide and sustain my actions every day. When I am troubled, confused, anxious, or unhappy, I can become quiet and open myself to the healing power around me. When I am given opportunities to act honorably toward myself and others, I honor my Higher Power by doing so. All right action, I believe, is a form of worship. We honor God when we honor what is good in us and in each other. When I can't live up to these ideals, I can be gentle and forgiving with myself, changing the things I can and turning the rest over to my Higher Power.

Sharing Recovery

Addiction is a lonely place. We are disconnected from ourselves, others, and the experience of a Power greater than ourselves. Recovery is a shared experience. We learn how to reconnect, to become whole. We don't have to be alone in recovery; it is always, everywhere, being shared by others like us who are learning how to be free.

If there is a single message in my story, it is that *we do not, and we cannot, recover alone.* Addiction is a terrible, destructive, pervasive disease that touches everything in our life. It wounds and distorts, fragments and isolates. Recovery is surrender to the healing power that connects us with our inner self and each other. I believe this healing power flows constantly among recovering people. Whenever and wherever we come together, we are shown the ways to open ourselves up to the possibilities of recovery.

I can never fully express my gratitude to those who have shared their journey of recovery with me. Writing this book has been a way for me to begin. Whatever I have learned and am learning has been through the freely given love of others. To you who are reading this, I pray that you, too, are able to share healing connections on your recovery journey.

THE TWELVE STEPS OF
ALCOHOLICS ANONYMOUS*

1. We admitted we were powerless over alcohol — that our lives had become unmanageable.

2. Came to believe that a Power greater than ourselves could restore us to sanity.

3. Made a decision to turn our will and our lives over to the care of God *as we understood Him.*

4. Made a searching and fearless moral inventory of ourselves.

5. Admitted to God, to ourselves, and to another human being the exact nature of our wrongs.

6. Were entirely ready to have God remove all these defects of character.

7. Humbly asked Him to remove our shortcomings.

8. Made a list of all persons we had harmed, and became willing to make amends to them all.

9. Made direct amends to such people wherever possible, except when to do so would injure them or others.

10. Continued to take personal inventory and when we were wrong promptly admitted it.

11. Sought through prayer and meditation to improve our conscious contact with God *as we understood Him*, praying only for knowledge of His will for us and the power to carry that out.

12. Having had a spiritual awakening as the result of these steps, we tried to carry this message to alcoholics, and to practice these principles in all our affairs.

* The Twelve Steps of A.A. are taken from *Alcoholics Anonymous* (Third Edition), published by A.A. World Services, Inc., New York, N.Y., 59-60. Reprinted with permission.

Other titles that will interest you . . .

Letting Go of Shame
Understanding How Shame Affects Your Life
by Ronald Potter-Efron and Patricia Potter-Efron
This book helps us identify our shame and the biological, psychological, and cultural factors that produce and reinforce it. Practical exercises guide us through the process of understanding our shame and taking positive action to heal ourselves. 192 pp.
Order No. 5082

Take What Works
How I Made the Most of My Recovery Program
by Anne W.
Anne W. lends her insight to some standard program truths, which are accepted without question, and perhaps should not be. She shares how coming to terms with these sayings helped her to expand and enrich her recovery program. 75 pp.
Order No. 5412

JourneyNotes
Writing for Recovery and Spiritual Growth
by Richard Solly and Roseann Lloyd
Learn how keeping a journal will help you get in touch with your feelings and clarify your spiritual values. Writing instructors Richard Solly and Roseann Lloyd use poetry, lists, and letters to help you create your own journey of self-discovery. 217 pp.
Order No. 5079
